Ghost Towns of North Mountain

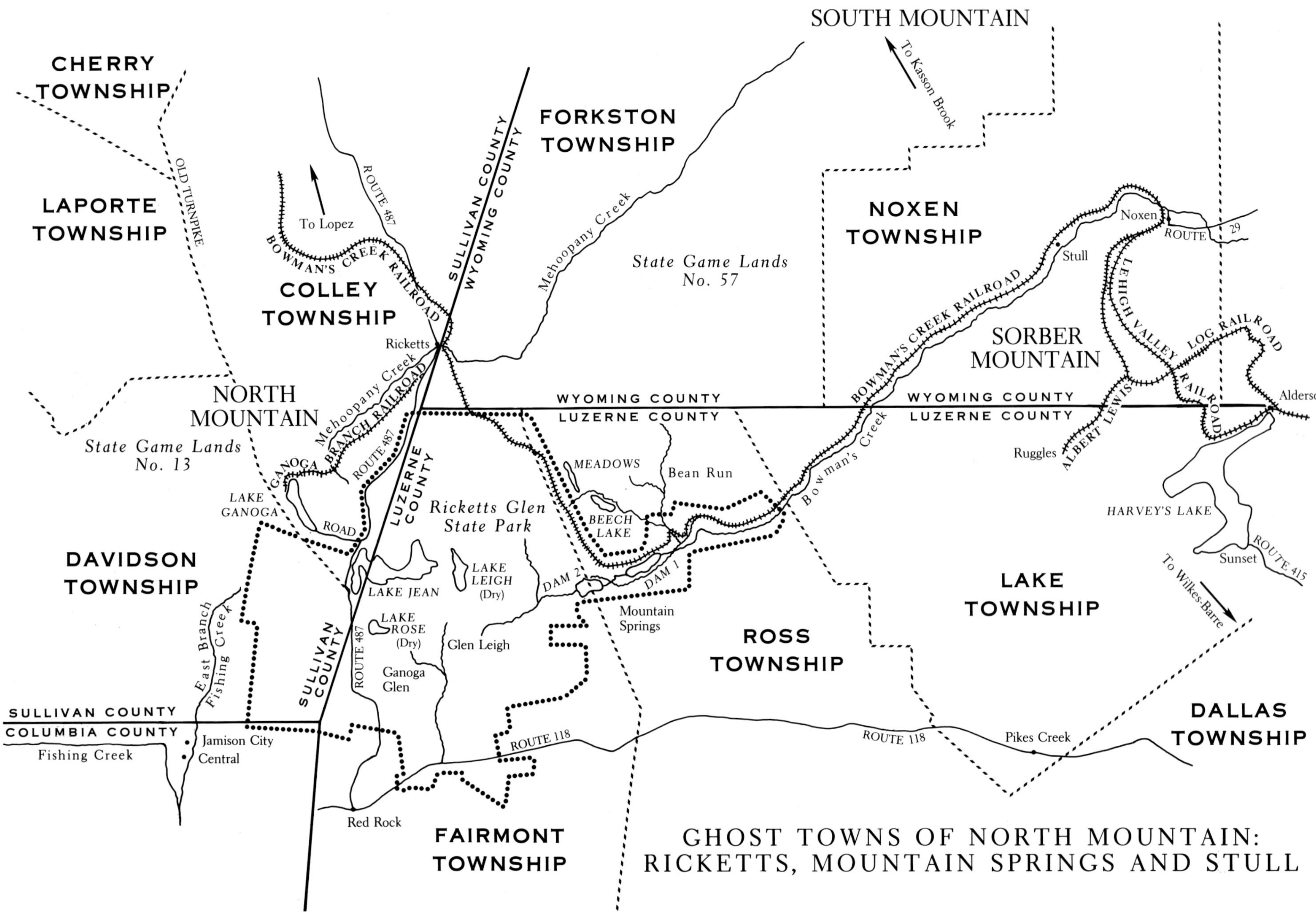

GHOST TOWNS OF NORTH MOUNTAIN:
RICKETTS, MOUNTAIN SPRINGS AND STULL

GHOST TOWNS OF NORTH MOUNTAIN

RICKETTS, MOUNTAIN SPRINGS, AND STULL

F. Charles Petrillo

Wyoming Historical and Geological Society
Wilkes-Barre, Pennsylvania 1991

Published by the Wyoming Historical and Geological Society
49 South Franklin Street, Wilkes-Barre, Pennsylvania 18701

Funded in part by the Edith Reynolds Trust

Second printing May 1992

Designed and composed by The Bookmakers, Incorporated, Wilkes-Barre, Pennsylvania
Printed and bound by Quinn-Woodbine Incorporated, Woodbine, New Jersey
Cover printed by Zodiac Marketing Services, Wilkes-Barre, Pennsylvania
Manufactured in the United States of America

ISBN 0-937537-00-4

FRONT COVER PHOTOGRAPH: *The sawmill at Ricketts in a photo postcard by Ranald Douglas, circa 1909. The log railroad is pitched slightly to permit the logs to fall off the railroad cars and into the log pool.*

REAR COVER PHOTOGRAPH: *A raft of ice is poled at Dam No. 1 at Mountain Springs in the late 1920s in this photograph by John Jennings, a professional Wilkes-Barre photographer. The raft will be cut into standard-sized floats nearly thirteen feet square, and the floats then cut into thirty-five ice cakes, each 32 x 22 inches. Paul Maransky holds the ice hook while manager Robert A. Stull is bundled up in business clothes on this breezy cold day.*

OPPOSITE: *Ranald Douglas in a cartoon self-portrait.*

To the Memory of

RANALD DOUGLAS
(1853-1910)

The Ricketts Photographer

Contents

List of Maps

Preface

While researching the history of Harvey's Lake for an earlier work, I encountered century-old articles noting the creation of the towns of Ricketts, Mountain Springs, and Stull, industrial communities unfamiliar to me. Certainly, I, too, have enjoyed Ricketts Glen State Park. But I was not aware of its rich history, or indeed the saga of Col. R. Bruce Ricketts, until I took a park-sponsored tour of the ghost town of Ricketts with Jay Krothe, park naturalist, and Chet Siegal, former state forester, both of whom I now appreciate as friends and fans of Ricketts lore. Chet formerly worked for William R. Ricketts at the Ganoga estate and has been singularly responsible for preserving Col. Ricketts' memorabilia. Chet has been extraordinarily trusting with me and we now share a unique enthusiasm in preserving the history of Col. Ricketts.

In a quest for more information on lumbering at Ricketts, I discovered the incredible work of Thomas T. Taber III of Muncy, and his associates, Walter C. Casler of Corey, and Benjamin F.G. Klein, Jr., of Strasburg. Their thirteen-volume work *Logging Railroad Era of Lumbering in Pennsylvania* is a state-wide history of the lumbering industry in the logging railroad era. The several pages they devoted to Ricketts and Stull in *Ghost Lumber Towns of Central Pennsylvania* stimulated an interest for a fuller treatment of North Mountain lumbering and suggested the title for this work. Similarly, the now scarce *The Quiet Boomtown* by Bloomsburg University professors Craig A. Newton and James R. Sperry, while a model work for the history of Jamison City, only mentions the Ricketts operation in a couple of pages. The work of these earlier writers has been partly adapted for this larger study.

Mountain Springs also deserved its own treatment to honor the many hardy men who devoted several decades in icy mountain winters to a fascinating industry along Bowman's Creek. A fine series of articles in April 1967 by Doris Harvey Wiant, who continues to care for the family's wonderful Wiant Museum near Sweet Valley, in *Country Impressions* (now *Suburban News*) was an excellent introduction to Mountain Springs. Members of the Kitchen family, Glenn A. Kitchen, Malcolm Kitchen and Mary Louise Buckalew, have been very helpful and understanding with me—and patient, since this work was promised five years ago. The mechanics of ice-cutting were even more difficult for me to understand than those of lumber milling.

Stull may have been completely forgotten had not the late Albert (Burt) Stitzer of Shavertown, who formerly worked at the mill town, collected the few surviving photographs of the town and encouraged the *Dallas Post* to publish them in the 1960s. *Step by Step*, a Noxen history by Janet Schooley, was also helpful. A debt too is owed to the late Roy A. Transue and the Transue family for assistance with Stull, and George Buckingham of Braintree, Massachusetts, for information on Ricketts. Similarly, Maj. Harry Owens, the late Paul Casterline, and the late Daniel A. Waters provided information on the Bowman's Creek Railroad.

Arthur A. Stull, son of Arthur L. Stull, and I have enjoyed several conversations in Washington, D.C., and his kindness and generosity in sharing Lewis and Stull family history and photographs is reflected in this work.

Additional thanks certainly must be extended to Col. Ricketts' granddaughters Elizabeth Ricketts Sterling, Esther Ricketts Stiles, and Swan McLean Grant who have shared their family record and good will with me.

The Edith Reynolds Trust has been very generous to the Wyoming Historical and Geological Society, and I trust this work merits the confidence they have in the society's programs and publications.

Foster Brooks of Mehoopany has graciously shared his photographic talents with me, and his interest and time, and contributed to this work with his support and friendship. He has helped save the precious photographic record of the region and the memory of Ranald Douglas.

Most important, the late J. Edward Smith of Montrose in every sense has co-authored the Ricketts work with me. In the early 1960s, Ed researched the history of several lumbering towns in the Endless Mountains, collected photographs, summarized a decade of various newspaper articles, and interviewed now deceased residents of the lumber towns. To narrow his research, he concentrated on Ricketts; he has shared all his enormous work with me. The map of the town of Ricketts was his creation after years of studying the town. Ed envisioned a fictional narrative of Ricketts told by a backwoods hick, but I am not so gifted a writer. Ed walked the Ricketts site with me, and we spent several special times together as he brought the town alive again. I must admit I really never understood the mechanics of milling or locomotives of which Ed was a master. Consequently, any defects in this work are certainly my own. There have also been too many times this summer of 1990 where I still needed his guidance. But Sue Smith has been as generous as Ed in sharing his collection with me to again review and it helped enormously.

As much as this work should be dedicated to Ed, we agreed Ranald Douglas deserved the honor. Ranald Douglas (1853–1910) was a deaf photographer who traveled from Orange, New Jersey, to the Mehoopany area about 1893. He made photographs of school children for a living. Whether he was deaf from birth or from an illness later in life is not known, nor is the extent of his speaking ability now known. By the early 1900s he settled in the area and made postcard photos of Ricketts, Lopez, Lovelton, Mehoopany, and Forkston. Far too little is known of Ranald Douglas. For a time he had a shop at Lopez; he also had a shack at Ricketts, and he took the log train to the lumber camps to make photos. He also was engaged by Col. Ricketts to take photos of the Ganoga estate.

The photo and scenic postcard was a national craze in the decade before World War I. Douglas scraped a living from postcard photography in the Endless Mountains. A good-natured man, he died on July 29, 1910, in Forkston and was buried by the local poor directors in an unmarked grave in the Forkston Cemetery. With the publication of this work, a suitable marker will be erected to him at the gravesite. Ranald Douglas also deserves a separate history of his photographic work. With few exceptions, Douglas's photos are the only photographic history to capture the town of Ricketts in this work, and without him the visual history of Ricketts would have been lost.

Summer 1990

F. Charles Petrillo
Wilkes-Barre, PA

Ghost Towns of North Mountain

Introduction

The rural and mountainous area surrounding Ricketts Glen State Park, at the intersection of Luzerne, Wyoming, and Sullivan counties, is known as North Mountain. The mountain range forms a watershed between the north and west branches of the Susquehanna River. At Ricketts Glen, Bowman's Creek begins to flow generally eastward through the now deserted ice-cutting town of Mountain Springs, along the former lumbering town of Stull, beyond the old tannery town of Noxen, into the farming valley of of Beaumont, and onward to the Susquehanna River below Tunkhannock. North of Ricketts Glen, Mehoopany Creek flows northeasterly through the ghost lumber town of Ricketts, eventually flowing into the Susquehanna River at the town of Mehoopany, another old lumbering center.

In central Sullivan County, Loyalsock Creek descends from World's End State Park and passes through Lopez, once the county's major lumbering center. The Loyalsock then flows into the west branch of the Susquehanna River. In lower Sullivan County, west of Ricketts Glen, Fishing Creek descends into a valley to Jamison City on the Sullivan–Columbia County line, also the site of a former lumbering community.

In the two decades between 1890 and 1910, the North Mountain area was the scene of the last major lumbering era in our region. Lumbering was the economic basis for the towns of Alderson (1887–1912) at Harvey's Lake, and at Stull (1891–1906) on Bowman's Creek, and for large lumbering operations in the towns of Lopez (1887–1905) on Loyalsock Creek, Jamison City (1889–1912) on Fishing Creek, and at Ricketts (1890–1913) on Mehoopany Creek.

Ice-cutting was another North Mountain industry during this era, with its major center at Mountain Springs (1891–1948) along Bowman's Creek, and to a smaller extent at Lake Ganoga (1896–c.1915), a private lake development near the state park. The ice industry continued to operate for another three decades after the end of lumbering in North Mountain, closing as mechanical refrigeration came into general household use immediately after World War II.

The Lumber Industry

The American lumber industry began in Maine in 1634 and was centered there for two hundred years, but in the 1830s New York State became the early nation's lumbering leader. In 1860, Pennsylvania, with over 28 million acres of land area, most of which was densely forested, became the industry leader. From 1870 to 1890, Michigan was the leading lumbering state. But between 1870 and 1890, Pennsylvania was still among the nation's top three lumber producers, and was fourth in 1910.

Pennsylvania's forests were initially stripped for white pine, in great part for the nation's ship-building industry. Prior to 1880, the principal means of transporting felled timber was by rafting or log drives on the state's rivers and streams. For a time, Williamsport (1838–1919), on the West Branch of the Susquehanna River in Lycoming County, was the "lumber capital of the world," utilizing log drives down the river until 1909 to Williamsport mills.

By 1885, lumber companies were increasingly using small "logging railroads" to reach into Pennsylvania's forest lands. Portable steam mills were also developed to be constructed in the forest lands. Both developments lessened the dependence of the industry on stream-side mill sites for water power. At the same time, the Pennsylvania lumber industry was greatly revived by the quest for hemlock, particularly for the bark from hemlock trees, which was an important source of the chemical tannin, used in the leather industry.

The production of leather goods from animal hides also grew into a substantial American industry during the nineteenth century. Between 1850 and 1899, the nation's tanning industry grew from $40 million to $200 million in value, with major industry conglomerates emerging by the end of the century.

The vast hemlock forests in Pennsylvania generally were not cut in the 1860s and 1870s. With the value of hemlock recognized in later decades, logging production for hemlock, remaining pine, and other timber increased greatly in the state. Indeed, capital investment in the state's lumber industry grew from nearly $11 million in 1860 to $24 million in 1870, to $45 million by 1890, when nearly 2,000 lumber mills still peppered the state's forest lands. The number of mills had declined from 3,700 in 1870, because of larger mill operations and consolidation of land ownership by timber land speculators.

In our region Sullivan and Wyoming counties were covered by vast timber tracts supporting only small lumbering operations until the late 1880s and early 1890s when the towns of Jamison City, Lopez, Stull, and Ricketts were created by major lumbering firms to harvest the forest lands. In the more populous Luzerne County, drained by the Susquehanna River, anthracite mining became the principle industry. However, lumbering was significant at Harvey's Lake on the Hollenback Estate lands during the 1840s through 1870s, and also during the 1870s through 1880s by John P. Crellin and Albert Lewis in the White Haven and Bear Creek region, which was drained by the Lehigh River and its tributary streams.

In the 1890s, a major lumbering industry was revived at Harvey's Lake and extended along Bowman's Creek by Albert Lewis, the "lumber king of Wyoming Valley." He was also tied financially and by his first marriage to the Crellin family and the Lehigh Valley Railroad. Lewis was also associated with Adam Stull and his son Arthur L. Stull in the Bowman's Creek lumber business.

A contemporary of Albert Lewis was the remarkable Col. Robert Bruce Ricketts, after whom Ricketts Glen State Park is named. Ricketts Glen State Park annually attracts over 375,000 visitors. Few are aware that a century ago the park and its surrounding game lands were the site of a major lumbering industry with a town, named Ricketts, of 800 residents. At Lake Ganoga, adjacent to the park lands, Col. Ricketts had a summer resort served by the Ganoga Branch of the Lehigh Valley Railroad.

A Civil War hero, Ricketts was an immense land speculator in the timber lands of Luzerne, Sullivan, and Wyoming counties. Col. Ricketts once owned nearly 60,000 acres in the region. Much of his land was principally drained by Mehoopany Creek. Ricketts' immense tracts were generally called his "Mehoopany Lands." Ricketts was on the verge of financial disaster for two decades until the Lehigh Valley Railroad was constructed through his lands. In the early 1890s, the Trexler and Turrell Lumber Company created the town of Ricketts, a few miles north of Lake Jean, which was a "boom town" from 1890 to 1913. Today it is a ghost town without a single marker to note its existence.

Through Col. Ricketts' foresight, the precious Kitchens Creek glens and waterfalls were preserved in their natural state and are the heart of Ricketts Glen State Park. Two-thirds of the 13,050-acre state park is former Ricketts land. Ricketts also protected his "pet," the Lake Ganoga area, from lumbering and only in the present generation is development truly occurring at the private Lake Ganoga development.

The Ice Industry

Prior to the 1830s, food was generally preserved by salting, spicing, pickling, or smoking. Butchers slaughtered meat only for the day's trade, as preservation for longer periods was not practical. Milk and dairy products and fresh fruits and vegetables subject to spoilage were sold in local markets since storage and shipping farm produce over any significant distance or time was not practical. Indeed, milk was often hauled to city markets at night when temperatures were cooler. Ale and beer making required cool temperatures and its manufacture was limited to the cooler months.

The early ice industry was localized. Farmers cut small harvests from local ponds, and only better homes, taverns, and hotels purchased ice from local dealers. Ice was a luxury not commonly available to the general public except for cooling drinks.

Urbanization, improved ice-box technology, and consumer demand, including the popularity of mineral waters, fruit juices, and ice cream, stimulated the creation of an American ice industry. Farmers increased their use of ice for meat and dairy use. Food cooled with ice could be shipped by railroad to more distant places. During the last half of the nineteenth century, ice became a necessity for home and business, and by the 1870s there were substantial ice dealers in medium-sized communities like Wilkes-Barre and Scranton.

The first commercial ice dealer in Wilkes-Barre was Capt. Gilman Converse, captain of the *Wyoming*, a 155-foot steamboat which hauled freight and passengers on the Susquehanna River from 1849 to 1852 between Tunkhannock and Pittston, with occasional trips to Wilkes-Barre. Gilman sold ice from 1855 to 1865, cutting it from the river and local ponds. After Gilman's business was destroyed in a March 1865 flood, he was succeeded by the Wilkes-Barre Ice Company, which was followed by the Wyoming Valley Ice Company in 1869.

By 1880, an estimated 5 million tons of ice was consumed by

the American public. Pennsylvania was the nation's third largest producer of ice, following Maine and New York. Pennsylvania consumed about 1 million tons annually, cut on the state's lakes and rivers or bought from Maine and New York ice firms. The industry, by this time, also supported major conglomerate ice firms; the most well-known was the Knickerbocker Ice Company of New York, which also reached into Pennsylvania. With the growth of the ice industry during the 1880s, substantial regional companies were formed in White Haven and Pocono Lake.

Albert Lewis and Arthur L. Stull were the founders of two major ice production companies in Luzerne County. In the mid-1890s, Lewis and Stull jointly founded the Mountain Springs Ice Company in Ross Township, located now in state game lands adjacent to Ricketts Glen State Park. Lewis left the Mountain Springs company in 1912. Stull, along with his brother Albert A. Stull, and a son Robert A. Stull, then managed the Mountain Springs Ice Company. Lewis owned an even larger ice company at Bear Creek, near Wilkes-Barre, where he lived in a tudor mansion amid a unique company town.

This work offers a history of Albert Lewis and Arthur L. Stull and their creation of two Bowman's Creek towns, Stull and Mountain Springs. In addition, the story of Col. Robert Bruce Ricketts and the lumbering town named after him on Mehoopany Creek is explored.

Albert Lewis and Arthur L. Stull

Albert Lewis (1840–1923)

Albert Lewis was the son of Abijah Lewis, a successful lumberman of Maine and Canada. The father married Alzare Romaine of Montreal, and the couple was living there when Albert Lewis was born in 1840. The family later moved to Beaumont in Wyoming County where Abijah Lewis lumbered and tutored his son in the business. Subsequently, the family relocated to Bucks Township where Abijah Lewis acquired timber lands by 1850, and a mill in White Haven in 1852.

At that time, the Lehigh Valley Railroad was building a railroad between Mauch Chunk (now Jim Thorpe) and White Haven to serve the rapidly developing coal, canal, and lumber industry along the Lehigh River. Young Albert Lewis obtained work as a timekeeper on the railroad in White Haven. His diligent work gained the attention of the powerful Asa G. Packer, the millionaire magnate of the Lehigh Valley Railroad system, who permitted Lewis to take charge of the first train to run between Mauch Chunk and White Haven. Lewis subsequently became the chief train dispatcher in White Haven where he continued to cement potentially lucrative relationships with the railroad's hierarchy. Lewis married Elizabeth (Lizzie) E. Crellin (1853–1885), a schoolteacher in Mauch Chunk. She was the daughter of John P. Crellin, who became the largest private landowner in White Haven, and the major lumber merchant to the Lehigh Valley Railroad. Crellin was married to Sarah Blakeslee, half-sister of Asa Packer's wife.

Lewis was able to avoid the service in 1864 during the Civil War because his railroad and lumber work was deemed essential to the Union War effort. Under the Civil War draft law, a "rich man's provision" permitted the hiring of a substitute to serve for a person conscripted by the Union. In Lewis's case, James Bryer, an Irish immigrant who worked for Abijah Lewis in the lumber business, served Lewis's duty.

Bryer served gallantly in the Union containment of Richmond, Virginia, the Confederate capital, and against Fort Fisher, North Carolina, a major southern supply depot. Wounded at the end of the war, Bryer returned to White Haven and presented Albert Lewis with a Civil War pistol. Lewis assured Bryer that he always had employment with his company.

In his late twenties, Lewis left the Lehigh Valley Railroad and acquired his first timber tract in Dennison Township in 1866. In the early 1870s, he began purchasing White Haven lands in earnest; by 1880 he was also purchasing land in Bear Creek. His timber tracts and mill sites along the Lehigh River, Hickory Run, and Bear Creek would soon total 30,000 acres. By 1870, he was associated with Allentown partners in timbering at White Haven. Lewis initially rafted logs on the streams and river in the Lehigh Gorge with a small force of men. He later constructed logging railroads from the forests to his mills to reach the main line of the Lehigh Valley Railroad. He was also a partner in the Glen Summit Hotel, which was principally owned by the Lehigh Valley Railroad. The hotel opened along the Lehigh Valley Railroad line between White Haven and Wilkes-Barre in February 1884.

In 1876, Lewis and Lehigh Valley Railroad investors purchased 13,000 acres along Bowman's Creek, between Harvey's Lake and Ricketts Glen, from Col. R. Bruce Ricketts, who owned immense timber lands in Wyoming and Sullivan counties and the northwestern corner of Luzerne County. But the Lehigh Valley Railroad did not complete a railroad through the tracts until the early 1890s.

On August 11, 1885, Lizzie Crellin Lewis died at the Glen Summit Hotel after a long illness. Lewis erected a memorial, the beautiful Grace Chapel, which still stands at Bear Creek adjacent to the Lewis's private cemetery. There were no children from this marriage.

During the late 1880s and early 1890s, Lewis built a railroad from Wyoming Valley to Harvey's Lake, where he opened a lumber business at the village of Alderson. With business associates Adam and Arthur L. Stull, and the backing of the Lehigh Valley Railroad,

Albert Lewis (1840–1923) and his wife Lily C. Lewis (1868–1950) are shown on a boating cruise in later life at an unidentified location.

the lands purchased in 1876 along Bowman's Creek were also opened to lumbering with the founding of the towns of Noxen and Stull. Ice production followed on the lakes Lewis and Stull built along Bowman's Creek above Stull.

During a business trip to England, Lewis met Lily Constance Westendert of London, whom he married there in September 1892. Her grace complemented Lewis's charity, and they were both recognized as national social figures. Lewis was known as "the lumber king." Children also affectionately called him "Daddy," as he had a life-long habit of giving shiny new dimes (and later quarters) to youngsters.

Albert and Lily Lewis had a summer home in Newport, Rhode Island, and a winter home in St. Augustine, Florida, but their principal residence was a palatial tudor residence in Bear Creek. The Bear Creek dam and lake were one of several Lewis had constructed to serve his Bear Creek Ice Company which he formed in March 1895. It was the major business enterprise of his later life.

By 1910, ice production was America's seventh largest industry. The Bear Creek and Mountain Springs operations were major contributors to the industry in the mid-Atlantic region. Lewis employed 125 men in his ice business in Bear Creek, which was a unique company village. Harvey's Lake and Bowman's Creek lumbering had ended in 1912, and the Lewis and Stull partnership was dissolved. Arthur L. Stull continued with the ice business on Bowman's Creek and Albert Lewis concentrated on his own ice plants at Bear Creek, outside of Wilkes-Barre.

The Bear Creek village was a social mecca for Lewis's influential and wealthy business network. Former Presidents Theodore Roosevelt and William Howard Taft each visited Lewis's estate in Bear Creek. The village also contained rent-free cottages where Lewis's fortunate employees lived, many of whom were immigrants. Lewis even supplied electricity to the homes from a powerhouse he constructed. He provided free housing at the village and other necessities to the aged and retired James Bryer, Lewis's Civil War substitute.

Lewis had his work force construct over one hundred miles of red-shale riding trails and driveways through the forests around Bear Creek. He had a personal stable of twenty-one fine driving horses. Lewis had an aversion to automobiles which were forbidden on his private roads. Beginning in 1894, Lewis had the Old East End Boulevard constructed as a toll road, but automobiles were not allowed on it until 1907, when the Wilkes-Barre Automobile Club finally persuaded Lewis to sell it and it became a county road. In later years Lewis, too, became an automobile fan.

On December 18, 1923, Albert Lewis died at the age of eighty-five in Bear Creek following a three-week illness. His showcase home had been destroyed in a fire six months earlier and a new Bear Creek home was only partially completed when he died. By the time of his death, his lumbering interests had been played out, but his ice industry was a huge success. In the winter of 1922–1923, his Bear Creek Company had shipped 100,000 tons of ice and would continue to operate until 1938.

The Lewis legacy today is primarily Bear Creek village, a private home development, and Bear Creek dam which preserves a Lewis ice lake.

Arthur L. Stull (1862–1942)

Arthur Lewis Stull is widely regarded as the most prominent member of the Stull family connected with Albert Lewis and the lumbering and ice-cutting operations at North Mountain. But Arthur L. Stull's father, Adam Stull (1833–1909), was the actual founder of the Stull family enterprise. Adam Stull was the son of Lewis and Elizabeth Guinter Stull. Lewis Stull (1797–1867) settled in Bucks Township in 1817 on a 166-acre farm. Lewis and Elizabeth Stull had nine children; eight grew to adulthood, but a son, John Stull, died in the Civil War. The other children became well-known in the regional business and agricultural communities.

The heavily forested area along the Lehigh River where the Stulls settled became a major lumbering region. Adam Stull entered the lumber business along the Lehigh, as did a brother Albert who later founded a lumber business in Lackawanna County. Adam Stull married Melvania Lewis (1836–1896), the oldest daughter of Abijah Lewis, and two of their four children, Arthur L. Stull and Albert A. Stull (1871–1946) would work with their father Adam in the lumber business. Another family member in the lumber business was William R. Stull, a son of Daniel Stull, another brother to Adam Stull. William Stull, who died in 1918, was married to Eliza Lewis, another daughter of Abijah Lewis. William Stull was a shareholder in the Bowman's Creek Lumber Company, the Albert Lewis Lumber and Manufacturing Company, as well as the Bear Creek Ice Company; but he was principally the manager of the Preston Lumber and Coal Company in Oakland, Maryland, in which Lewis and the Stulls had joint interests.

Adam Stull was the brother-in-law of Albert Lewis and both spent their young manhood along the Lehigh River. In 1870, Stull became a manager in Lewis's lumber business in White Haven. Adam Stull relocated to Alderson in Harvey's Lake in the late 1880s when Lewis opened the Harvey's Lake and Bowman's Creek area to lumbering. Stull and Lewis were very close friends and associates until the latter's death in November 1909.

Arthur L. Stull was intimately associated with his father, Adam, and his uncle, Albert Lewis, in the lumber and ice business. He attended Wyoming Seminary, and upon graduation at the age of eighteen, he was employed by Albert Lewis as a timekeeper in the lumber business at Bear Creek until 1887. When Lewis opened the Harvey's Lake and Bowman's Creek lumber district in 1887, Arthur L. Stull was named superintendent of the Alderson lumber mill operations. In August 1890, Stull became the general manager and treasurer of the Albert Lewis Lumber and Manufacturing Company, which was extending its operations to the new lumber mill in a town named Stull. Within the next few years, Stull was managing ice-cutting at two artificial lakes (Mountain Springs) built at Bean Run above Stull. Both Stull and Mountain Springs were along Bowman's Creek. Until 1902, the Albert Lewis Lumber and Manufacturing Company was only operating under a lease from the Bowman's Creek Lumber Company to timber the 13,000-acre tract purchased from Col. R. Bruce Ricketts in 1876. In May 1902, the Bowman's Creek Company sold its land holdings for $87,996 to the Albert Lewis Lumber and Manufacturing Company.

Arthur L. Stull is shown circa 1918.

In August 1907, the Albert Lewis Lumber and Manufacturing Company was reorganized to provide Arthur L. Stull a partnership interest in the company. The company controlled 22,400 acres in Noxen and Monroe townships in Wyoming County and Fairmont, Ross and Lake townships in Luzerne County. Albert Lewis retained a three-quarter interest in the lands, with Arthur L. Stull a one-quarter owner in a partnership titled Lewis and Stull. Adam Stull was seemingly retired from the business.

The Lewis and Stull arrangement continued business operations in Alderson, Stull, and Mountain Springs, but by the years 1911 and 1912, the lumber tracts were nearly exhausted. The ice-cutting industry, however, was still booming, but apparently relations had strained between Lewis and the Stull brothers, Arthur L. and Albert A. Stull, particularly after the death of Adam Stull in 1909.

In December 1912, the Lewis and Stull partnership was dissolved. Lewis retained 15,000 acres in Noxen, Forkston, Lake, Ross, and Fairmont Townships—now played out for lumbering purposes—and Arthur L. Stull retained 6,800 acres encompassing the Mountain Springs and Beech Lake ice plants and the Alderson property at Harvey's Lake, a substantial business with three decades of life left to it. By this time, too, Albert Lewis was seventy-two and was content to oversee his incredibly active Bear Creek ice plants, spending his winters in Newport, or more likely, St. Augustine, where he was also a notable social figure and community benefactor. In early 1927, three years after Lewis's death, his heirs sold the tracts Lewis had retained in 1912 to Arthur L. Stull and his brother Albert A. Stull. Five years later—in 1933—the Stull brothers and Robert A. Stull, a son of Arthur L. Stull, created a separate partnership to operate the ice business at Mountain Springs. The Stull family also operated a supply store at Alderson for some time and they sold considerable real estate from their holdings. The Stull farm at Harvey's Lake was sold to State Senator Andrew J. Sordoni in 1931–1933.

On May 22, 1942, Arthur Lewis Stull died of a heart attack in Oakland, Maryland. Ironically, he had traveled there to attend the funeral of Atty. Frederick Thayer, a close friend and a prominent lumber dealer. Stull resided at 182 South Franklin Street in Wilkes-Barre with his wife Mary Edie Stull. An elder in the First Presbyterian Church, he was closely associated with the Salvation Army, serving on its board of directors for thirty years. Even earlier in 1901, he helped in the fund-raising campaign to build the original Salvation Army Citadel on South Pennsylvania Avenue in Wilkes-Barre. He was also a director of the Miner's National Bank (now the United Penn Bank).

The Stull lands in Wyoming and Luzerne Counties which were not sold to private interests have become state game lands adjacent to Ricketts Glen State Park. Stull's Ice Dam Number 2 (formerly Mountain Springs) is now Mount Springs, a lake owned by the Pennsylvania Fish Commission.

The Bowman's Creek Branch of the Lehigh Valley Railroad (1887-1963)

In 1869, the Lehigh Valley Railroad finished the construction of a 96-mile railroad line along the Susquehanna River from Wilkes-Barre to Waverly, New York. Called the Pennsylvania and New York Canal and Railroad Company, the railroad was largely built alongside the North Branch Extension Canal (1856–1872), which connected the Wyoming coal field in Luzerne County to a canal system in central New York to reach the Great Lakes. The canal itself was heavily damaged in an 1865 flood and was closed in 1872, after which the company double-tracked the rail line. But this railroad completely by-passed the rich timber lands of the North Mountain in Luzerne, Wyoming, and Sullivan counties. Prior to the early 1890s, lumber firms in the Bowman's Creek and Mehoopany Creek lands used splash dams, creek freshets or wagons to reach mills and local markets.

The absence of a railroad through the North Mountain range plagued its major landowner, Col. R. Bruce Ricketts, for a quarter of a century, and blocked his fortune-building from the unbroken forest lands he had acquired in three counties. Without a railroad, the existing lumber merchants in Sullivan and Wyoming Counties were limited to small milling and tanning operations, while the Wyoming Valley mining industry and growing mid-Atlantic cities clamored for lumber.

In time, however, various interests, under the eye of the Lehigh Valley Railroad, planned to connect Towanda with Wilkes-Barre by construction of a substantial railroad through the vast North Mountain forest. In 1867, the independent Sullivan and Erie Railroad opened a 24-mile line between Monroeton, five miles from Towanda, to Bernice, to reach the semi-anthracite mine fields of Bradford County. This coal had a market in New York State. Monroeton was connected to Towanda on the Susquehanna River by the Barclay Railroad, later known as the Susquehanna and New York Railroad, over which the Lehigh Valley would later have trackage rights. The Sullivan and Erie had financial difficulties and was reorganized, after foreclosure in 1874, as the State Line and Sullivan Railroad. In 1884, the State Line and Sullivan Railroad was leased to the Pennsylvania and New York Canal and Railroad Company.

In 1884, the Loyalsock Railroad, corporately controlled by the Pennsylvania and New York, was chartered to build a 32-mile extension from the State Line's terminus at Bernice, to Bowman's Creek near Bean Run (Mountain Springs), which would open up both Lopez and Col. Ricketts' North Mountain lands. This line opened in 1893 as part of the through line between Wilkes-Barre and Towanda. There was additional mileage to the State Line and the

Loyalsock lines representing small branches to outlying mill and resort towns. For example, two of the most important on the Loyalsock were the 7.75-mile branch connecting Thorndale on the main track with the lumber town of Lopez, and the 3.85-mile Ganoga Branch connecting the lumber town of Ricketts with Col. Ricketts' Lake Ganoga resort.

The last important railroad link was the connecting railroad from Ricketts at North Mountain to Wilkes-Barre on the Susquehanna River. This link was the Wilkes-Barre and Harvey's Lake Railroad. The Wyoming Valley mining industry centered in Wilkes-Barre had an insatiable demand for timber to be used for breakers, mine railroad ties, and support lumber in hundreds of miles of mine tunnels. The Wyoming Valley also had main-line railroad connections to haul lumber to Allentown, New York, and Philadelphia markets, where immigration and industrialization pressures demanded lumber for housing and factories.

The Construction Years

In 1883, the Lehigh Valley Railroad surveyed at least three different routes from the Wyoming Valley to Harvey's Lake and Bowman's Creek to reach the North Mountain lumber tracts. There also was interest by the Pennsylvania Railroad Company in a similar line, and at least a rumor of interest by the Delaware, Lackawanna, and Western Railroad Company. But no firm action was taken by these major railroads to construct a railroad in the early 1880s, even though the Lehigh Valley had purchased 13,000 acres of Bowman's Creek timber lands in 1876, through which the railroad from Ricketts' lands to Harvey's Lake could be built.

Albert Lewis and his Lehigh Valley friends were surprised in October 1885, when a group of local investors, generally representing Wyoming Valley lumber, insurance, and ice interests, under the leadership of John S. Shonk, George W. Shonk, and A.S. Orr, incorporated the Wilkes-Barre and Harvey's Lake Railroad Company. They planned to build a railroad from the Wyoming Valley through the Back Mountain community of Dallas, to the newly developing resort at Harvey's lake. The investors were initially divided as to inviting Albert Lewis to join the corporation. But the capital necessary to purchase the right-of-way and to construct a railroad was heavy. Lewis had both an interest and the financial resources to help Shonk's friends, and Lewis joined the investors. Lewis immediately recognized the importance of controlling the railroad to serve the Bowman's Creek lands which he and his Lehigh Valley Railroad investors had purchased a decade earlier. Within a year, the new railroad found itself $90,000 in debt to Lewis for advances made by Lewis to acquire the right-of-way through the Back Mountain for the railroad. By June 1886, some original stockholders in the railroad had sold out to Lewis who then installed his own financial and legal friends and advisors as owners of the railroad.

Lewis employed a large number of East European immigrants, 300 men, to complete the railroad which reached Dallas in December 1886. He planned to headquarter his Back Mountain lumber business at the north corner of Harvey's Lake, which became the village of Alderson, named after William C. Alderson, treasurer of the Lehigh Valley Railroad.

The Albert Lewis Lumber and Manufacturing Company had two locomotives during the course of the lumbering industry at Alderson and Stull. The first locomotive was the D. P. Cope, which was named after Lewis's railroad construction boss. The locomotive is shown pushing a carload of bark, probably to Noxen on the single-track log line of the company.

On May 26, 1887, Lewis improvised a flat car for passenger use and ran a special excursion for friends to enjoy a party at his Alderson estate, where he had built a showpiece log cottage near the site of the sawmill he would build the following winter. The cottage was a major attraction for many years and would become the lake home of Adam Stull, Lewis's chief associate in the lake's lumber business. Regular passenger service on the twelve-mile Luzerne to Harvey's Lake railroad began on June 16, 1887.

On August 5, 1887, Lewis sold the twelve-mile Harvey's Lake railroad to the Lehigh Valley Railroad. By August 16, 1887, two trains each way began a daily run to the lake. In October 1887, the Alderson post office was created for the growing North Corner. Edward Bush, the first postmaster at Alderson, was the freight agent for the Lewis lumber company at the lake.

From Alderson, Lewis also constructed an additional eleven miles of log railroad to Bowman's Creek at Noxen. Apparently, the Lewis log train road was the original track for an extension of the Wilkes-Barre and Harvey's Lake Railroad Company from Alderson to the Bowman's Creek timbering fields. But the grades for the log roads were too difficult for the heavier trains of the Lehigh Valley Railroad. The Lehigh Valley Railroad instead began to construct a new six-mile rail bed from Alderson to Noxen on a different route more suitable for passenger and freight service.

Lewis maintained the original line of his log train to tap the timbering tracts along Bowman's Creek. The Lewis log train ran west directly from Alderson and would link with the new Lehigh Valley line at Beaver Run immediately below Noxen. From the log train line to Noxen, Lewis built a spur in March 1889 to Ruggles, where Lewis had purchased the J.J. Shonk lumber mill.

The second locomotive of the Albert Lewis Lumber Company was simply called No. 2. The photograph appears to be taken at the Alderson lumber yard at Harvey's Lake. The men are Adam Bill, engineer; Harvey Miller, conductor; Erwin Franks, brakeman; and Jack Hartley, brakeman.

The Harvey's Lake railroad began in Luzerne on the west side of the Susquehanna River. Prior to 1891, there was no direct line from Wilkes-Barre to the lake. A separate Lehigh Valley Railroad train had to be taken on the east side of the river in Wilkes-Barre at 10:00 a.m., north to Pittston Junction. There, a transfer was made to a Lackawanna and Bloomsburg train which crossed from the east to the west side of the river. The train then returned down river to Bennett's Crossing at Luzerne before it connected with the Harvey's Lake railroad. As a better alternative, Wilkes-Barre passengers to the lake initially could take a trolley from Public Square and cross the river to Kingston and then take a short ride on the Lackawanna and Bloomsburg railroad to Luzerne to connect to the Harvey's Lake railroad. In either case, the connections were very cumbersome and time-consuming. To return on the railroad from the lake, passengers had to leave the Alderson station at 3:00 p.m. This awkward schedule left only a few hours for tourists to enjoy the lake, and service on the Harvey's Lake railroad was not profitable. The railroad quickly planned a more economical route and the construction of a large amusement park at the lake to attract additional passenger service.

An eighteen-mile direct line from Wilkes-Barre to Alderson at Harvey's Lake became available in 1891 when the Lehigh Valley Railroad constructed the Port Bowkley bridge across the river above Wilkes-Barre from Plains to Forty Fort. The piers of this railroad bridge can still be seen from the Cross Valley Expressway which crosses the river below the old railroad bridge. The direct line at Port Bowkley, in 1891, coincided with the construction of mills and tanneries at the "boom towns" of Noxen and Stull, and also with the opening of the picnic grounds at the lake by the railroad.

By July 1891, the new Lehigh Valley track at Harvey's Lake was carried an additional mile along the lake shore from Alderson to the picnic grounds where a small Harvey's Lake substation was

The Stull motor launch is shown at a dock at Alderson with the Albert Lewis sawmill in the background. In the photograph, left to right, are Albert A. Stull, Adam Stull (with beard), Fred Glasby, Carol Harvey, and Robert A. Stull. The launch was named after Selma Utz Stull, wife of Albert A. Stull.

located. By April 1892, the track was completed to Bowman's Creek at Noxen. Nearly seventeen miles to the west was Ricketts, another lumbering "boom town." Ricketts was connected to Towanda by 43 miles of track operated by the Loyalsock Railroad and the State Line and Sullivan Railroad Company, subsidiary lines of the Lehigh Valley Railroad. Only eight miles of additional railroad between Noxen and Bean Run below Ricketts was required to connect Wilkes-Barre with New York State through the North Mountain.

Lewis constructed the missing link in the summer of 1892. By September 1892, there was a direct rail line between Wilkes-Barre, Harvey's Lake, and Towanda. However, the direct line between the Wyoming Valley and Towanda was not in use. There was a dispute between Lewis and the railroad company over the purchase price of Lewis's vital link, and also over the rates the railroad would charge Lewis to use the line to haul timber.

In the meantime, a critical telegraph line needed to manage two-way traffic on a single-track system was not constructed. Negotiations were slow and a hard winter with high snow delayed the telegraph line until late spring. Freighters and the general public in the Wyoming Valley berated the company and Lewis and clamored to have the new railroad opened. By May 1893, the Trexler and Turrell Lumber Company had opened their mill at Ricketts and had cut five million feet of logs which were ready to be hauled out by railroad, and 7,000 tons of bark were piled for shipment to the Noxen tannery. In late June 1893, Lewis and the Lehigh Valley finally reached an accord and the line was ready to open, but not without incident.

On June 24, 1893, a special excursion train ran over the new line

The Mountain Railroad

Come, now, and listen to what I may say,
There is something wrong—there's too much delay;
And all that I ask is your careful attention,
And something of interest I think I can mention,
Through an evergreen forest of tall stately trees—
By fine gushing fountains and mountains' pure breeze,
A railroad was built, as its presence now shows,
But for what purpose constructed, the Lord only knows.
The rails, they are quiet—the sleepers lie still,
And the whole thing is as useless as a Dallas saw mill;
And why all this waste of muscle and means
Of crossing high mountains and wild mountain streams
And left there to rot with no show of life?
It seems quite as silly as crossing seas for a wife.

And when will it start? Can anyone tell?
It seems as dead as the stock of Glen Summit Hotel.
But why should this road so useless remain?
Everything is completed why not run the trains?
The cause of the delay asked by one—asked by all,
It seems as great pity, there's plenty to haul.
There's bark and there's logs in quantity here
Besides lumber to ship that would last the whole year.

Almost anywhere else would receive prompt attention;
And there's passenger travel that would be a nice thing,
If the company would only put life in the thing.

I am like many others and would like to know
Who is the boss of the business and won't let it go.
Some say it is Lewis that sprags the machine
And if that is the case we will say that it's mean.
Some say it is Sayre, as he has some stock
In a boundary of hemlock that is not on the Sock;
Though it is my opinion, and I wish to be fair,
It's my opinion it's Lewis, it's my opinion it's Sayre
As they own the timber on the side of the hill
That is very convenient to the Stull Lewis mill:
For it does look as though they were in the ring
With their very short haul that's a mighty nice thing.
But how about those like Turrell and Kipp?
They both have saw mills and lumber to ship;
And there's Jennings Bros., who have a large mill,
Have to ship around Cape Horn what orders they fill.

I could mention others, and there are quite a number,
That must ship around the Horn when they market their lumber.
And now I am through, but who could not swear
That something is wrong and mighty unfair;
And as that is the case, you see what they do,
They discommode many to favor a few.

This poem by an anonymous author appeared in a Wilkes-Barre newspaper on April 13, 1893, and lampoons the delay in opening the Bowman's Creek railroad.

from Wilkes-Barre to Towanda. In addition to Lewis, the train carried officials from the Lehigh Valley Railroad and Reading Railroad, the latter for a time operating the Lehigh system. Twenty miles beyond Harvey's Lake the excursion collided with a log train operating for the Trexler lumber firm. Lewis Hunsinger, a train hand for Trexler, was caught between falling logs and had a leg severed. The lumber train had been warned to switch off to a siding until the special passed, but after waiting a time, the log train re-entered the main line and attempted to reach another siding further along the line when the collision occurred. The two locomotives were badly damaged and the train officials were delayed until another engine could be brought to the scene.

Finally, on July 1, 1893, the Lehigh Valley Railroad acquired the complete line which provided direct rail service from the Wyoming Valley through the booming timbering fields of Luzerne, Wyoming, and Sullivan counties, and on to Towanda. The 79-mile railroad was named the Bowman's Creek Branch of the Lehigh Valley Railroad. Closed circuit telegraphs were used by the railroad and its train dispatchers to manage operations—particularly important on a single-track operation like Bowman's Creek.

By agreement with the railroad, Western Union services were also available on the same telegraph line, tying together the rural villages with each other and with larger cities. Money transfers, too, were available by telegraph. Stations had their own distinctive telegraph call letters: Wilkes-Barre (WD), Dallas (D), Alderson (DR), Noxen (NX), Stull (UX), Ricketts (RI), and Lopez (OZ). Towanda had two wire service designations: DP for freight, and DA for the passenger office.

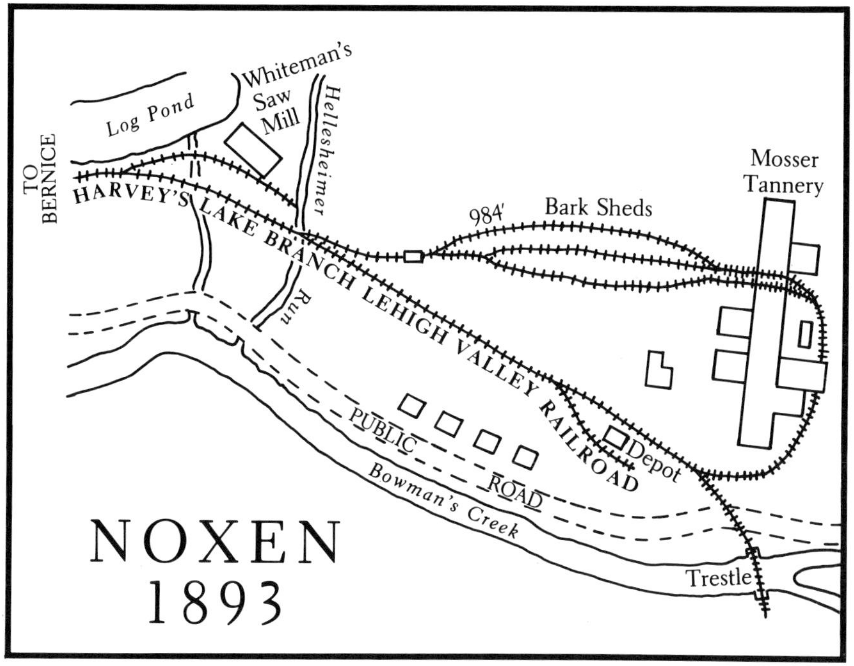

Harvey's Lake Ice Industry

An interesting sidelight to the history of the Albert Lewis Lumber and Manufacturing Company and the Bowman's Creek Railroad is why the Lewis company did not develop a major ice-cutting industry on the 658-acre Harvey's Lake, where Lewis had manufacturing facilities and access to a railroad. In fact, Albert Lewis did

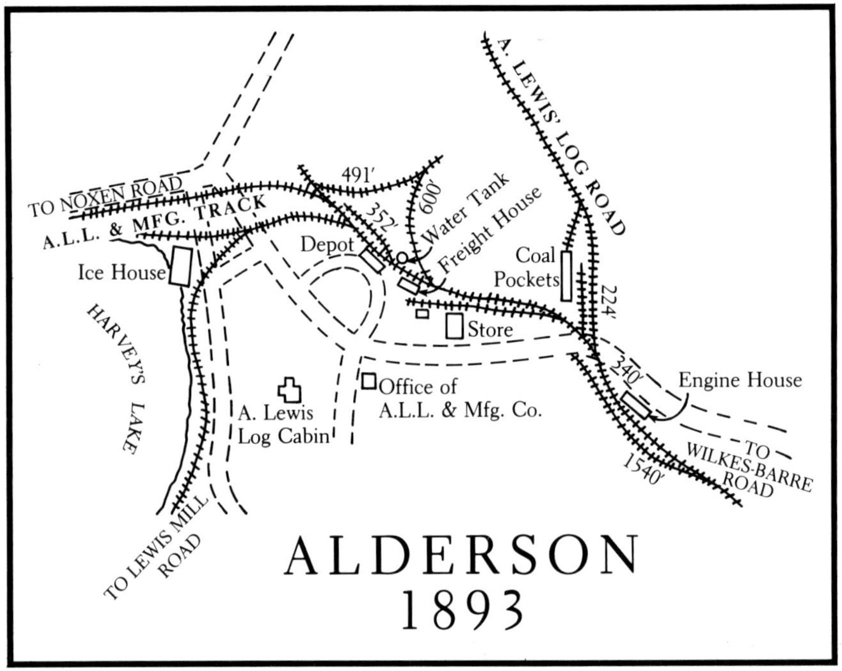

attempt ice-cutting at the lake, but he was thwarted by a peculiar land issue involving the bottom of Harvey's Lake.

In the fall of 1870, Hendrick B. Wright, a Wilkes-Barre lawyer, mine owner, and local congressman, who was attracted to the lake and later built a home there, and Charles T. Barnum, a local judge who also lived at the lake, applied to the state for ownership rights to the land underneath Harvey's Lake, which had not been included in any previous state grants. Land grants to areas under rivers and lakes in the state were not uncommon, particularly to support mining rights. The lake bottom was divided into two large parcels, and on October 13, 1870, the state granted Wright a warrant for 285 acres and Barnum a warrant for 329 acres. The lake was surveyed on November 3, and state patents were issued to Wright and Barnum on February 20, 1871.

Although access to Harvey's Lake was limited by a three or four-hour stagecoach ride, public interest and access to the lake for fishing and resort purposes was important to Wyoming Valley residents. The lake patents drew the anger of local residents who protested to the legislature. The legislature responded with a law declaring Harvey's Lake and Harvey's Creek to be navigable waters.

The effect of the state law was not to challenge Wright and Barnum's ownership of the land under the lake, but to assure access to the lake waters by adjoining property owners. In fairness to Wright and Barnum, they never intended to exclude public use of the lake. Wright and Barnum planned to engage in ice-cutting on the lake in the winter, and the lake patents arguably provided a legal basis to support the business. Wright and Barnum exchanged half interests in each other's lake patents, and they built four large ice houses in the Alderson corner for their ice business. Wright and Barnum did exercise a proprietary interest in Harvey's Lake by stocking it with 300 black bass, a new game fish, in late August 1871.

Wright and Barnum, however, did not enter the ice-cutting business themselves in any serious way, and the patents for the most part were not exercised. Wright died in 1881, and Barnum in 1887, and the patents fell to their estates and heirs to manage. In January 1888, the heirs of H.B. Wright and C.T. Barnum granted George R. Wright and Benjamin F. Barnum, sons of the original patent owners, a license to cut ice on the lake. The license, however, was then leased to Albert Lewis who planned to cut at least 6,000 tons of ice annually at the lake, with a royalty to the heirs of Wright and Barnum.

From 1888 to 1893, the Albert Lewis Lumbering and Manufacturing Company cut ice at Harvey's Lake. The ice houses were in Alderson on the corner near the Alderson church. In March 1889, for example, the Lewis company had fifty men at the lake working in the ice industry there. Ten to twenty railroad cars were loaded daily, each with twenty to thirty tons of ice. Older Wright and Barnum ice houses were filled, and two new houses, 40 by 80 feet, were also being filled while still under construction, each holding 15,000 tons of ice blocks.

The Lewis ice operations at Harvey's Lake only lasted a few years. The Wright and Barnum heirs were not pleased with their business arrangement with Lewis. Their royalty from the Lewis ice contract in 1893 was only $60.75, and they had an undisclosed dispute over his business methods, which probably shaved their royalties to a meaningless venture. In November 1893, the license with Lewis was cancelled. Lewis quickly developed a new ice industry at Bean Run (Mountain Springs) and at Bear Creek.

The Wright and Barnum heirs leased the ice rights to Theodore Renshaw of Plymouth in the 1894 and 1895 seasons. Afterwards the heirs unsuccessfully sought to sell the lake patents. They abandoned the ice-cutting business, and seemingly, too, a claim to the patents, and in February 1900 the uninsured Barnum and Wright ice houses were destroyed by fire. For the next 45 years, small individual firms cut ice on the lake, ignoring the lake patents.

The Village of Alderson

Alderson was an extremely active village on the north corner of Harvey's Lake from 1887 to 1912. The Lewis sawmill in Alderson was operating by April 1888. The railroad depot served countless tons of freight in addition to passenger traffic. Steamboats provided passenger service from the Alderson station to hotels and boarding houses, which were dotted along the lake. Particularly well-known were the Rhodes Hotel (1855–1908), Lake Grove House (1881–1897), and its successor, the magnificent Hotel Oneonta (1898–1919), all located at the Sunset section of the lake. Alderson had its own school and church on lots contributed by the Albert Lewis Lumber Company. The Lehigh Valley picnic grounds, later known as Hanson's Amusement Park, were a mile down the lake from Alderson and the railroad passed through the park grounds.

W.H. Rauch was the foreman at the Alderson sawmill. Sawmills were initially equipped with huge circular saws, about six feet in diameter, to cut timber. In 1889, the bandsaw was generally introduced in American sawmills. A bandsaw was an endless band of steel with cutting teeth on one or both sides. The bandsaw was draped over a lower and upper wheel. A bandsaw forty-feet long by nearly a foot wide was installed in the Alderson mill in the early

Only the rooftop of the Alderson train station is in view as the D. P. Cope pulls a flatcar of lumber. Regular Lehigh Valley passenger cars are idle at a siding. The Lewis log line juts westward from the lower right to the lower left of the photograph. In the rear center is the Lewis and Stull company store. The photograph was taken in 1892 by Wilkes-Barre photographer C. F. Cook for a photo series of Harvey's Lake.

1890s to replace a circular saw. A bandsaw cutting path was only one-eighth of an inch wide compared to the three-eighths of an inch path of a circular saw, saving one inch of board for every four cuts of a bandsaw. At Alderson, Joseph Trutchler was the chief sawyer responsible for the 400 razor-sharp teeth of the bandsaws. Broken teeth were quickly cut out by Trutchler, who, aided by red-hot tongs, clamps, and silver solder, would add new teeth to the bandsaw. At any one time, thousands of logs filled the boom on the lake by the Alderson mill.

There was enough lumbering in the Harvey's Lake and Bowman's Creek region to support both the Stull and Alderson sawmills until the Stull mill burned in 1906. The Alderson mill continued at least until 1912 when the last tract near the lake was cut. Lewis and Stull, the partnership which ran the mills, was dissolved in late 1912. Thereafter, the Stull interests continued at Harvey's Lake and Bowman's Creek in the farming, ice, and land business. The Alderson sawmill was dismantled about 1918.

The Railroad's Decline

Twenty years after the Bowman's Creek Branch opened to traffic, a number of factors were quickly ending the profitability of the railroad. A trolley line to the Sunset section of Harvey's Lake (1898–1931) drew away passenger service from Alderson, except for train excursions to the lake's amusement park. After World War I, young people increasingly moved from the farms to cities and were drawn away from country living. The automobile age also had arrived; cars were quicker and more convenient than scheduled trains. Not only passenger service, but also freight service declined. The old State Line and Sullivan Railroad was dependent on haulage from the semi-anthracite coal industry in Bernice, which increasingly lost its market. By 1913, the major lumber business was over at Ricketts, Stull, and Alderson. The Lopez mills, too, were closed between 1905 and 1907. Any further lumbering was limited to small lots, particularly for mine props, which were hauled by truck. The ice industry at Mountain Springs and the tannery at Noxen continued, but mechanical refrigeration, artificial ice, and leather substitutes were making severe in-roads into these industries.

By the mid-1920s, there was little passenger traffic on the Bowman's Creek Branch. The twice daily passenger trains were reduced to one train each way daily on December 19, 1928. A passenger train from Wilkes-Barre to Towanda left Wyoming Valley at about 8:00 a.m. A similar train from Towanda to Wilkes-Barre left at 10:00 a.m. During the middle of the day, a local freight train running west to Bernice would place cars at sidings along the route and unload freight. The return freight train picked up ice cars in Mountain Springs, and local freight arrived in Wilkes-Barre about 8:00 p.m. Yet, the Bowman's Creek line was the only substantial transportation available to handle passenger and freight service for tiny villages along the creek between Noxen and Ricketts Glen. Roads were few and crude. Separate passenger and freight trains to Alderson were discontinued on April 2, 1934, and the last advertised passenger service, even to the resort of Harvey's Lake, appeared in March 1936. In 1938–1939, the tracks between Lopez and Mountain Springs were removed.

For another dozen years, the Lehigh Valley Railroad sought to close Bowman's Creek and its other marginal railroad lines, but community pressure often kept smaller lines open. Finally, however, in 1948, the Interstate Commerce Commission permitted the

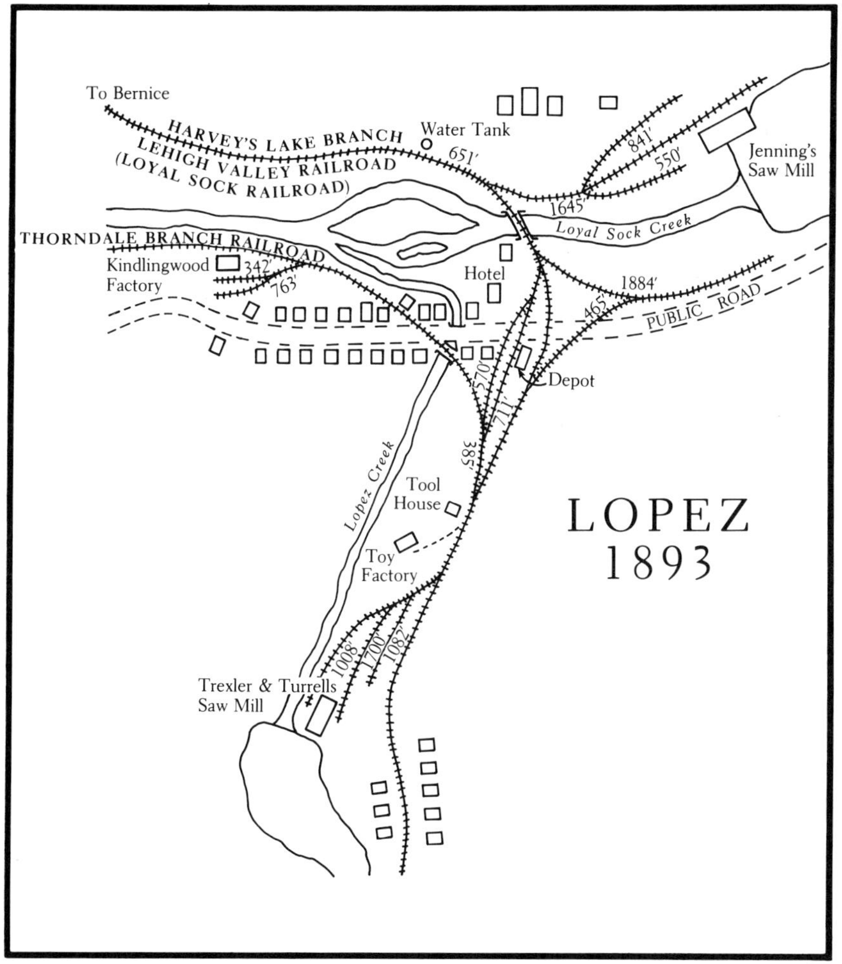

Lehigh Valley Railroad to close traffic above Noxen on the Bowman's Creek Branch. During the next fifteen years, after the ice industry closed at Mountain Springs, the Bowman's Creek Branch limped along, with one freight train daily in its last years. In fact, the entire Lehigh Valley Railroad system was in severe trouble.

In July 1963, the Interstate Commerce Commission authorized the Lehigh Valley Railroad to abandon the Bowman's Creek Branch line between Dallas and Noxen. The railroad had been in severe financial difficulty for years, and passenger service along the entire Lehigh Valley Railroad system had ended as a practical matter in 1961. Mechanical refrigeration had ended the ice-cutting industry after World War II and eliminated the hauling of ice cars by the railroad, although the railroad had continued to haul hides to the Noxen tannery. The tannery, however, had peaked in 1941 when it employed 217 persons. When the tannery closed in 1961, it ended the last remaining freight service of any consequence along the Bowman's Creek Branch, and the last freight service on the Back Mountain line typically carried only a single boxcar. The Alderson station had already been removed in May 1958. Governmental approval to close the railroad line between Luzerne and Dallas was granted to the Lehigh Valley Railroad in September 1963. On Sunday, December 22, 1963, at 12:01 a.m., the Lehigh Valley Railroad formally abandoned the Bowman's Creek Branch from Luzerne to Dallas.

In 1970, the Lehigh Valley Railroad sought reorganization of its collapsing financial and operations structure under federal bankruptcy law. On April 1, 1976, the federal government's sponsored Consolidated Rail Corporation (Conrail) absorbed the Lehigh Valley Railroad.

Stull (1891-1906)

The town of Stull had its origin in the early land speculation of Col. R. Bruce Ricketts, the vast land baron of North Mountain, and Albert Lewis, the energetic lumber king of Luzerne County. Both were aware that the North Mountain and Bowman's Creek tracts could make them wealthy if exploited for their virgin timber.

Lewis may have been aware of the potential of the Bowman's Creek area from his childhood when his father settled at Beaumont, a village along the wild mountain stream. Ricketts, too, wanted to capitalize on his extensive land holdings and also to attract a railroad to the North Mountain. Lewis, of course, had the necessary connections with the Lehigh Valley Railroad, a coal and transportation empire.

On August 5, 1874, Ricketts agreed to sell 13,032 acres of prime Ricketts timberlands along Bowman's Creek in Luzerne and Wyoming counties to the 34-year-old ambitious Albert Lewis and six other Lehigh Valley Railroad associates. He retained a one- thirteenth interest in the lands hoping to use it as leverage in closing the final deal. Ricketts tried to entice the Lehigh Valley Railroad to purchase additional lands, including his Lake Ganoga property and the waterfalls which now grace Ricketts Glen State Park, in a proposed financial package, if the company would immediately build a railroad through North Mountain. But the railroad partners may have felt such a commitment was premature, or were not inclined to become too indebted to Ricketts. But Ricketts was in debt from his land purchases and he needed cash. The sale was finally closed on January 14, 1876, and the land deeded to the Lewis group for $120,000, approximately $10 an acre. Ricketts also relinquished his one-thirteenth interest in the tracts.

Without a railroad to the Bowman's Creek lands, however, the tracts lay dormant for a decade. Lewis was extremely active at this time along the Lehigh River and would soon enter the Bear Creek area, with the Bowman's Creek lands a reserve for future development. Meanwhile, Ricketts was trying to become a millionaire by selling his much larger remaining lands in Sullivan and Wyoming counties.

In 1885 Wilkes-Barre interests began construction of a railroad to Harvey's Lake; a railroad line to tap the Bowman's Creek lands was within view, which Lewis quickly seized to complete for the Lehigh Valley Railroad. At the same time, Lewis and his investors formed the Bowman's Creek Land and Lumber Company, Ltd., a partnership for certain tax advantages, to control the 13,000 acres purchased in 1876. Some recapitalization may have occurred when the company sold the lands in November 1886 for $260,000 to a corporation similarly named the Bowman's Creek Lumber Company. There also may have been some change in the investors at

The original mill of the Albert Lewis Lumbering and Manufacturing Company was built in the winter of 1890–1891 and was operational in May 1891. The Bowman's Creek Railroad runs along the north bank of the creek in the lower left hand corner of the photograph. The mill burned on April 7, 1902.

this time but Lewis was clearly still in control. The Bowman's Creek Lumber Company leased the lands to Lewis who would form the Albert Lewis Lumber and Manufacturing Company in August 1890 to exploit the timberlands. The lumber company was capitalized at $400,000 by Lewis and ten much smaller investors.

Following the sale by Albert Lewis of the twelve-mile Wilkes-Barre and Harvey's Lake Railroad to the Lehigh Valley Railroad in August 1887, Lewis completed construction of a ten-mile winding log train railroad to reach the village of Lewis, a hamlet on Bowman's Creek a few miles north of the lake, which would be renamed Noxen the following year. Lewis's log train line to Noxen was largely in place by January 1890. His line was used by Noxen manufacturers to reach the Lehigh Valley line in Alderson until late 1892, when a more direct alternate Lehigh Valley line from Alderson to Noxen was opened. Substantial new construction was underway at Noxen and it was evident that a new boom town on Bowman's Creek, about two miles above Noxen, was also under construction. Lewis had previously attempted to purchase a new sawmill under construction at Noxen by R.A. Whiteman, former Wilkes-Barre city treasurer, but Whiteman refused to sell. Consequently, Lewis may have created Stull in response to Whiteman's rebuff. A post office designation for Noxen was made in September 1888, and the new town above Noxen was named Stull, after Adam Stull, in March 1890 when a post office there was authorized. The name Noxen did not honor a person or site but was adopted because it was short and may have been suggested by the federal postal authority. Another story holds that during a town meeting a child saw a passing team of oxen and said, "Mommy, there goes a 'eam of N'oxen," and the townspeople adopted her misstatement as the town name.

The second mill at Stull was larger and had adjacent auxiliary buildings. This mill burned on November 22, 1906, signaling the end of the town.

During the winter of 1890–1891, the Albert Lewis firm built a sawmill at Stull. The area was formerly known for its trout fishing and hunting, but was now alive with the buzz of sawmills, the shriek of the locomotive, and the clapping of the woodcutter's axe. The Lewis mill was operating in May 1891. It was 130-feet long and 60-feet wide, with a reported daily capacity of 100,000 board feet of lumber. Stull was built along the narrow creek valley about a quarter of a mile upstream from a little village once known as Stonetown or Stone's Mills and named after Ben Stone, a local millwright and early settler who also became Stull's postmaster. He had been the principal local timberer in the area since 1872. Homes were now in the process of construction at Stull for the mill workers, wood choppers, and bark peelers.

By August 1891, the Whiteman mill at Noxen was also in operation along with the substantial Mosser tannery, which would be Noxen's principal industry for seventy years. George K. Mosser was a son of James K. Mosser of Trexlertown. The father had developed one of the major tanning firms in the mid-Atlantic region. The Mosser Tanning Company was chartered on June 17, 1890. Among the principals were members of the Mosser family and Albert Lewis. Lewis sold the company 72 acres for the tannery complex. Lewis also entered into an exclusive agreement to sell all the bark from the 13,000 acres he controlled to the Noxen tannery.

Within a year, the creek valley had grown from one dozen farm families to a lively 500, who were mostly employed in the Noxen and Stull industries. A.D. Kresge built a hotel at Noxen and was erecting a tin store, harness shop, and a barber shop. The Lewis mill in Stull was in full operation. Lewis also purchased the John

J. Shonk mill in Ruggles which Shonk lost in a February 1888 fire. By March 1889, Lewis constructed a branch line of his log railroad from Alderson to Ruggles where he rebuilt the mill. At this time, Lewis also acquired timberlands in Maryland and Crellin, West Virginia. Crellin was named after R.P. Crellin, one of Lewis's principal assistants and financial partners, and the brother of Lewis's first wife.

During the winter months, the Lewis crews were extraordinarily busy at both the Harvey's Lake and Stull mills. By March 1892, one million feet of logs were loaded in honeycomb fashion on the ice at Harvey's Lake and a log boom to contain them in the lake was under construction. Work began at 7:00 a.m. in the woods along Bowman's Creek, and all along the creek there were railroad ties to lay spur log lines to reach into the opening forests, while timber and cord wood were cut and hauled to the log railroad for shipment to the mills and Noxen tannery.

By December 1892, passenger trains ran twice daily between Wilkes-Barre and the Bowman's Creek communities. At Noxen, Ziba Sickler had a lock on the choice level land near the tannery, but the high price of his building lots were driving new mechanics and laborers to cheaper lots among the hills. Kresge's hotel was usually filled with traveling salesmen or boarders, and the enterprising hotel owner was now building a blacksmith and wheelwright shop. Near Whiteman's mill, a log slide was constructed to bring the fallen timber to the mill pond. A log slide is a trough made of timbers and could be a mile or more in length if needed. The cut timber was hauled to the slide by mules. Loaded on the slide, the timber would fall by gravity down the mountain log slide to a creek or mill site. Where the logs might run too rapidly, spikes could be driven up through the slide bottom to scratch the timber and slow down its descent.

Teamsters who drove the horse teams hauling timber are shown at the Stull log slide. Logs loaded on the slide descended by gravity to a rail site for shipment to the mill. A log slide could also carry logs directly to a mill pond. Noah McCloskey, the woods boss, is the first man on the left.

Adam Stull was the general manager of the Albert Lewis Lumbering and Manufacturing Company, with his son, Arthur L. Stull, as the principal assistant at the Stull mill. William Austin was foreman at the mill. Other key personnel were Charles Mitchell, saw filer; Charles Deubler, gang edger; James Newell, carriage sitter; Charles Dereamer, mill engineer; Archer Weiss, setter; Charles Thomas, night watchman and owner of a small store at Noxen; Frank Brittain, sawyer; Thomas Stout, log sorter; Joseph Bullock, shipper; and Al Lauderbaugh, fireman. Austin was formerly with Shonk's lumber mill in Ruggles and was brought to Stull when Lewis bought the Ruggles operation.

There was also a lath mill at Stull managed by Edward Transue, who came to Stull with three sons from Lewis's operations at Bear Creek. At the Stull mill, Ed Transue, Jr., became a saw filer, and Frank Transue was a sawyer, an important position supervising the sawing of lumber. In the woods, Noah McCloskey and Johnny Adams were notable "woods bosses." McCloskey was also associated for some time with the ice operations at Mountain Springs.

Stull also had a company store managed by S.S. Johnson and Fred Stull, a son of Adam Stull. They had formerly operated the Harvey's Lake Supply Company at Alderson.

The Stull mill and Noxen tannery operations increasingly drew additional laborers, mechanics, blacksmiths, wheelwrights, and other enterprises to the area. There were also smaller finishing mills owned by Ben Stone, E.H. Elston, and others, with additional Noxen hotels run by Thomas Dolan and Serfernis Hawk. Other retailers included Grant Van Campen, a coal dealer, and W.F. Brown, who had a store opposite the Kresge Hotel. At Stull, Hattie Thomas kept a boarding house for the mill workers.

In March 1896, fifty men worked at the mill itself. In the mill pond, workers sorted the logs; a circular chain from the pond drew the logs into the mill where the circular saw "squared" the logs, after which the squared log passed through a set of gang

Only a few Stull photographs have survived. This is a photograph of the Stull company store with Fred Stull in the foreground and Howard Dinstill on the store's porch.

These men worked around the Stull mill circa 1896. Left to right, front row, Fred Stull, Ed Transue, Sr., Charles Mitchell, Alf Lauderbaugh, Frank Britton, and John Stout; second row, Charles Deubler, Frank Transue, Tom Stout, Chance Beam, Bill Thomas, Frank Blossom, Jim Beam, George Brown, Herb Lasher, Jim Newell, Ed Transue, Jr., and Egbert Stull; third row, Jacob Huey, Harry Newell, Butler Edwards, Andrew Kocher, Charles Glance, Joe Bullock, William Austin, Garfield Transue, George Thomas, and Cal Transue. In the window is Hank Beam. The boys in the foreground are Max Mitchell, left, and Corey Austin, right.

saws which could cut the log into 500 board feet at one time. The typical output for Stull was 65,000 board feet daily, despite the mill's larger capacity.

Accidents and illness were common in the Bowman's Creek mill towns, keeping Noxen's Dr. Tibbins busy. William Wilson, for example, had a leg broken in March 1896 while hauling logs. A horse was killed in the same accident. In the same month, Llewelyn Thomas suffered a crushed leg which had to be amputated. In June 1897, a Mr. Smith, on his first day of employment, caught his foot in the endless chain at the Stull mill pond and amputation initially seemed necessary, but Dr. Tibbins saved it. Another mishap occurred in November 1899, when the Lewis log train jumped the track at Bean Run. John Hartly, an eight-year employee, jumped from the car to escape injury, but the car landed on him, severing one leg and almost the second; he also broke his hip. He died late in the evening at Wilkes-Barre General Hospital. Unsanitary conditions prevailed at some farms and homes, and deadly typhoid fever from poor water regularly occurred. Indeed, William T. Austin, the Stull mill foreman, died of typhoid fever in October 1899. He was also a school director at Stull and was largely responsible for erection of the Stull church.

Churches and schools were the most important institutions in rural areas. There was a rude school building at Stone's Mills in the early 1870s—it had no paint or plaster and the seats were

The Stull school children are shown in 1900. Professor Beishline is the first person on the left in row six; teacher Nellie Baker is the last person in row five. Emily McCloskey who became the post mistress at Mountain Springs is the next to the last child on the right in the first row. Albert F. Stitzer, who collected and preserved the Stull photographs in this publication, is the fifth boy from the left in row two.

hemlock benches. Rev. James Phoenix, a local farmer and Methodist-Episcopal preacher from Noxen, presided at services held at the school. When Phoenix became disabled from old age, Protestant-Methodists, under Rev. Joseph Anderson of Harvey's Lake, offered services at the old school and at the "white schoolhouse" which replaced it. In 1892, as Stull was developing, Mrs. B.M. Stone arranged for Centermoreland pastors to regularly provide services at the school. She also founded the Ladies Aid Society to raise funds for a church. They deposited $100 in the Rockafellow Bank of Wilkes-Barre, but lost it when the bank failed—a now forgotten, but then notorious, episode in local commercial history. The society was discouraged for a time, but subsequently raised funds for an organ and a pulpit bible. Rev. C.D. Skinner, a Wyoming Seminary student, was the pastor in 1893–1894, receiving $100 in salary.

The Noxen community had a similar, although earlier, church history. A church group was formed around the year 1840 on Bowman's Creek which met at an old log schoolhouse and later at a more distant red schoolhouse. Local pastors were Oliver Lewis, Abraham Frear, and James Phoenix. In 1883, services were relocated to a "white schoolhouse" in Noxen with a new church dedicated in December 1886 at a cost of $1,000.

In June 1896, Fred Stull organized a Sunday School at Bean Run, the ice-cutting town further up the rail line, later known as Mountain Springs. The Sunday School was presumably held at the Bean Run school. Since there was not a regular church as yet at Stull, the Bean Run Sunday School was served by a pastor from Noxen.

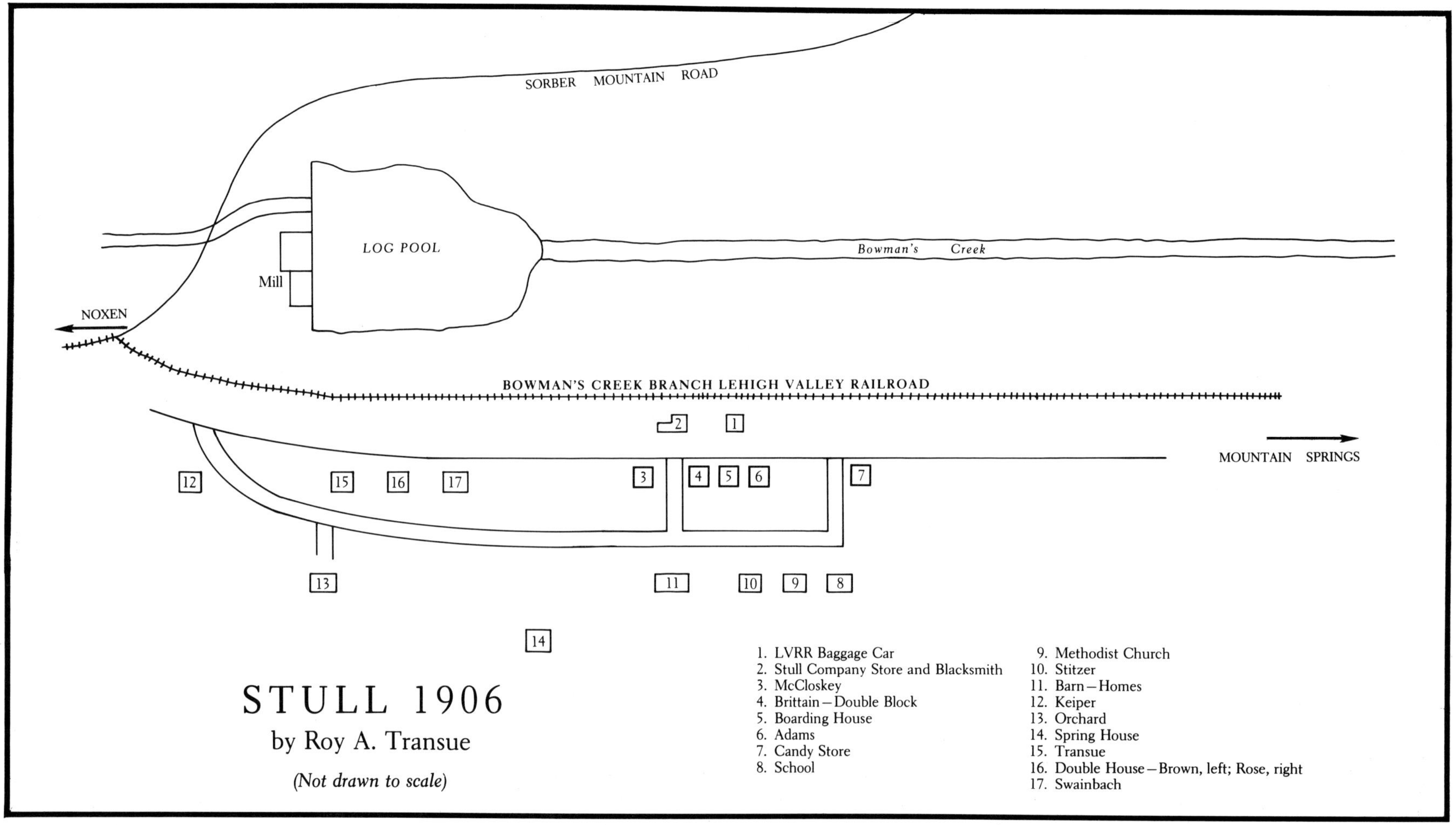
SORBER MOUNTAIN ROAD
LOG POOL
Mill
Bowman's Creek
NOXEN
BOWMAN'S CREEK BRANCH LEHIGH VALLEY RAILROAD
MOUNTAIN SPRINGS
1
2
3
4
5
6
7
8
9
10
11
12
13
14
15
16
17
STULL 1906
by Roy A. Transue
(Not drawn to scale)
1. LVRR Baggage Car
2. Stull Company Store and Blacksmith
3. McCloskey
4. Brittain—Double Block
5. Boarding House
6. Adams
7. Candy Store
8. School
9. Methodist Church
10. Stitzer
11. Barn—Homes
12. Keiper
13. Orchard
14. Spring House
15. Transue
16. Double House—Brown, left; Rose, right
17. Swainbach

Sentiment for a Stull church grew through the last years of the 1890s, and on Sunday, October 29, 1899, a new Methodist-Episcopal church was dedicated. The church lot was donated by the Lewis lumber company and built by men from the mill. The church was heated by a steam line connected to the mill boiler. The church trustees were Ed Transue, Jr., Frank Brittain, Charles Deubler, and William Austin. Unfortunately, the robust and well-liked Austin died immediately before the dedication.

The 24 by 32-foot Stull church cost $850, but was controversial because an earlier community committee apparently could have built a larger church for $750. Because of the dispute, some church members boycotted the dedication and did not contribute towards the last $80 needed to pay for its construction. Nevertheless, the church was full for a religious rally by the Epworth League. Prayer meetings were held on Wednesday evenings and a Sunday School was organized.

In Noxen, there were three churches serving the community. It was a local joke that Noxen needed three churches to keep the Noxen crowd in line. The growing Noxen and Stull area was originally part of Monroe Township in Wyoming County. However, on petition of the local residents, the Wyoming County Court approved the creation of Noxen Township on February 21, 1895, with township officials elected on April 13, 1895. A Noxen Township School Board was formed on June 3, 1895. Noxen was always the larger community. It had three schools in 1895, and a new four-room school opened in September 1897 with four teachers.

In July 1895, a new two-room, graded school at Stull opened with Professor Beal and Nellie Baker in charge, but in September 1899 Professor E.B. Beishline replaced Beal. Lillian Gordner would later replace Baker. Not all the Stull children who enrolled in school attended on a regular basis. The Stull school was crowded with 80 to 90 pupils in the late 1890s, shared by the two teachers. A degree of absenteeism apparently was common, however, which provided some relief to the teachers. Still, a significant number of students did not miss a day of school. By 1903, a three-year high school program was available at Noxen to area students, which older Stull students could attend.

In addition to the Stull mill, the immediate area also supported other mills. In the late 1890s, Trexler and Turrell, which had the second largest mill in the region at Ricketts, also had a smaller mill on South Mountain, north of Stull near Kasson Brook. Trexler and Turrell also had a mill at Noxen. The Trexler firm shipped its hemlock bark from Ricketts and South Mountain to the Noxen tannery and its men could easily switch work between Ricketts, South Mountain, and Noxen as available work required.

The community life of Stull was typical of a small, rural town. There were frequent, although simple, social gatherings such as ice cream socials and chicken suppers. Readings, recitations, and temperance lectures at the local schools drew a crowd, as would regular revival services. In February 1900, William Reinhart of Noxen had six students for mandolin classes which were held on Tuesday evenings at the Stull school. Most lumber towns also had a baseball team and a local band. A ladies aid society held sewing bees to repair or make clothes for destitute or ill households. Handmade quilts were also raffled to raise charitable funds.

For the men, hunting season provided a recreational outlet, with bear hunting a particular favorite. The woods surrounding Stull, then as today, were a haven for rattlesnakes, and there was some talk when Adam Stull killed a snake with fourteen rattles in mid-August 1899. In the winter, ice skating at Harvey's Lake was popular among the youth. The pool at the Stull dam was apparently not used for skating. Exhaust steam from the mill was diverted into the pool to partially clear the ice so work on the mill pond could continue in the winter.

Farming in the flat acres along the creek or in mountain patches was widespread. Oats and corn seemed to be the most common crops, along with hay. These crops fed the horse teams which worked in the woods. The hay was loaded loose in the summer on flat rail cars and taken to horse stables in Bean Run, South Run, and Alderson. There were also plum, cherry, and apple trees which freely served the community. Huckleberries and blackberries were in abundance and picked by the villagers.

Stull was regularly visited by traveling salesmen, better known as "drummers," such as James L. Vose of Tunkhannock, an insurance salesman, or Joseph Maltz of Towanda, who sold jewelry. Butcher and vegetable wagons regularly stopped in the town. Local farmers with excess produce took wagons as far as Wilkes-Barre to sell it. For a time, Noxen had its own newspaper, *The Weekly Vidette,* and correspondents from the farm and mill towns, Stull, Noxen, Beaumont, Centermoreland, and Harvey's Lake had their own columns in the weekly *Dallas Post.* These columns were mostly filled with innocent social news, such as weddings, births, family visits, guests, and trips. Indeed, visiting elsewhere, and entertaining friends at home, seemed the most common social activities—little different from rural community news columns ninety years later.

Saw mills were prone to disaster. The boilers were fired by sawdust and waste wood. A fire in the boiler room of the Alderson mill was discovered by Louis Frank, the night watchman, one Saturday night in late April 1898. Frank fastened down the whistle valve; a bucket brigade responded and prevented the fire from spreading to the mill itself, only thirty feet away. In March 1902, the Preston Lumber and Coal Company, in which Albert Lewis had an interest, lost a mill in Crellin, Maryland, in a fire.

On April 7, 1902, a fire began in the Stull boiler room and destroyed the sawmill. The flames had spread rapidly and the workmen who worked heroically were unable to save the mill. The Lewis firm built another mill at the same site. The second mill was substantially different in its construction, but news accounts do not appear to accurately describe it. One account stated that Lewis replaced the burned mill by relocating to Stull a mill that he owned in Mehoopany.

The second mill at Stull was rebuilt with a bandsaw, but the mill only lasted four years. On November 22, 1906, at 10:30 p.m., the night watchman discovered a fire in the mill's interior. The mill whistle was sounded and the workmen rushed to the mill. By midnight, it was obvious the mill could not be saved. The workmen directed their hoses to saving the lumber stock in the adjoining lumber yards. It was initially planned to rebuild the Stull mill again. However, the tracts were within a few years of depletion and the mill was not rebuilt. Rather, timber cut from the remaining tracts was hauled by railroad to the Lewis mill in Alderson.

The Stull community would only last a few more years. The remaining timber stands were few, and by 1911–1912, even the Alderson mill was within view of closing. The Stull school closed in 1912. Within months, Albert Lewis was no longer active in lumbering at Bowman's Creek or Harvey's Lake. He was making a fortune ice-cutting at Bear Creek, while the brothers Arthur and Albert Stull were concentrating on ice-cutting at Mountain Springs. The Stull mill ruins remained in place until 1918 when the remains were salvaged for iron scrap for the World War I effort, as was the Alderson mill. The town of Stull disintegrated and reverted largely to its pre-boom farming days. Today a few homes dot the hillside in old Stonetown, and Bowman's Creek quietly flows past the few mill foundations and memories where a generation once flourished.

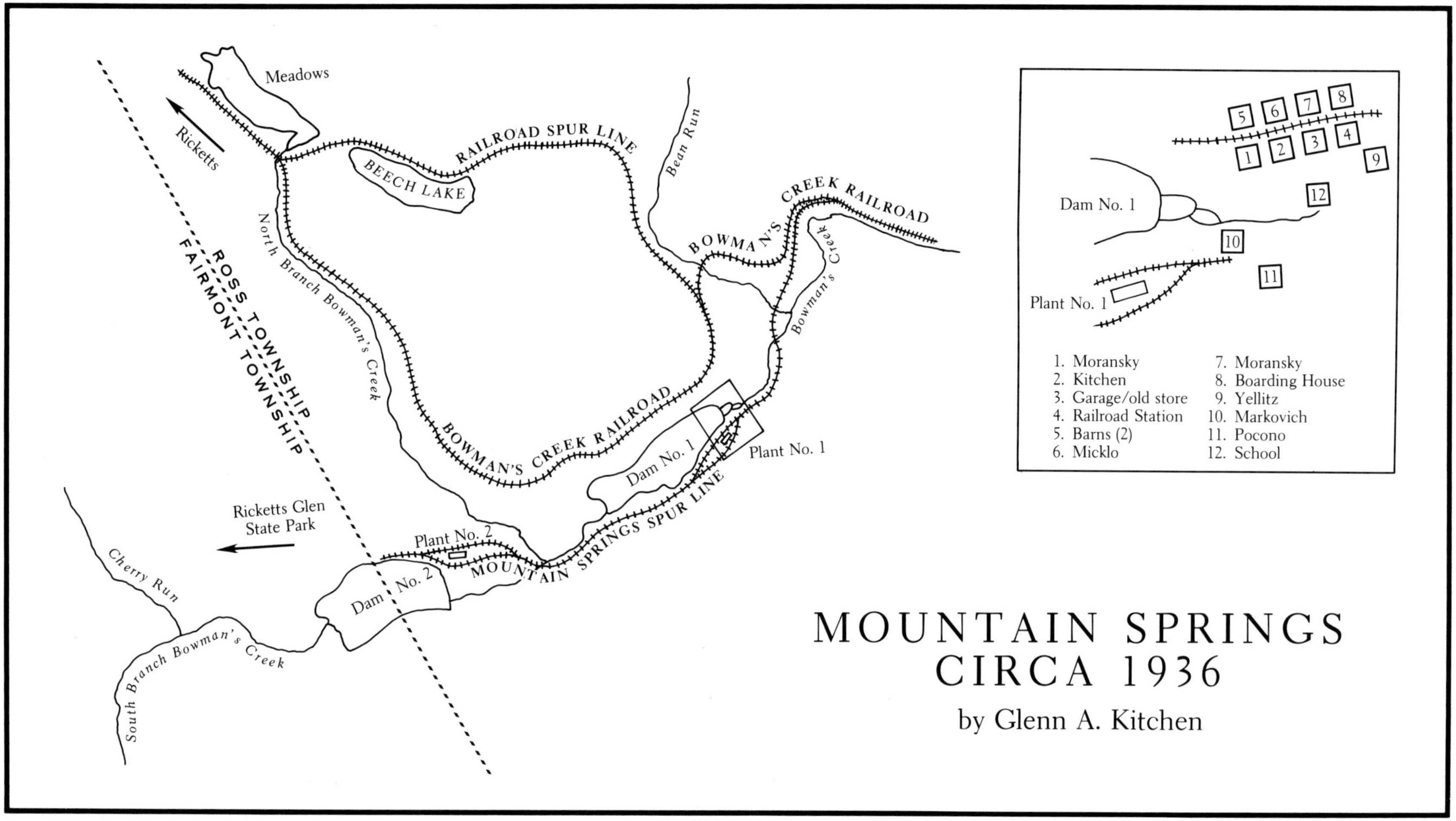
Meadows
Ricketts
RAILROAD SPUR LINE
BEECH LAKE
Bean Run
BOWMAN'S CREEK RAILROAD
ROSS TOWNSHIP
FAIRMONT TOWNSHIP
North Branch Bowman's Creek
Bowman's Creek
BOWMAN'S CREEK RAILROAD
Dam No. 1
Plant No. 1
MOUNTAIN SPRINGS SPUR LINE
Plant No. 2
Ricketts Glen State Park
Cherry Run
Dam No. 2
South Branch Bowman's Creek
Dam No. 1
Plant No. 1
1. Moransky
2. Kitchen
3. Garage/old store
4. Railroad Station
5. Barns (2)
6. Micklo
7. Moransky
8. Boarding House
9. Yellitz
10. Markovich
11. Pocono
12. School
MOUNTAIN SPRINGS
CIRCA 1936
by Glenn A. Kitchen

Mountain Springs (1890-1948)

The Early Years

The ice industry at Mountain Springs may not have been intentionally designed. Harvey's Lake would have been the natural site for a major ice industry, but the Wright and Barnum patents to the lake discouraged its development. Indeed, Splash Dam No. 1 at Bean Run was developed by Albert Lewis, not for the ice industry, but as an extension of his lumber industry at Stull downstream on Bowman's Creek.

In October 1890, the Albert Lewis Lumber and Manufacturing Company began construction of a log and timber dam on Bowman's Creek, near Bean Run, a small stream which runs into the creek. The initial dam site was a failure; the creek bed was too soft to support a dam. In October 1891, a second dam site just above Bean Run was selected and Splash Dam No. 1 was constructed. A stream, Meadow Run, runs into Bowman's Creek above the site, which helped to feed the small lake.

The original purpose of Splash Dam No. 1 was to create a forty-acre log pond into which felled timber was dumped from the railroad. Water released from the dam through a log chute could carry the timber on an artificial flood downstream to the mill pond 7.7 miles below in Stull. A successful splash dam would have lessened Lewis's dependence on, and charges for, the use of the railroad that he was constructing along Bowman's Creek for the Lehigh Valley Railroad. Apparently, Splash Dam No. 1 was used as a splash dam at least through 1895, but it was not successful. The fall in the creek was too steep and the twisting creek bed caused the released water to rush ahead of the logs, and too often the logs became stranded along the shore instead of being carried downstream to the mill.

With the completion and sale by Lewis to the Lehigh Valley of the railroad along the creek in 1893, a splash dam was not critical to carry the logs to mill. His company ran log railroad lines into the forest lands to haul timber to the Lehigh Valley line and then down to Stull. Lewis then converted Splash Dam No. 1 to ice-cutting in the mid-1890s, an industry he also formed at Bear Creek in 1895, particularly since Harvey's Lake was closed to him in 1893 for formation of a major ice industry.

The Bowman's Creek ice plant was originally called Bean Run. There are no statistics available regarding its early years nor is the date of its first ice-cutting certain, but probably it was the early months of 1896. Clearly the business was very successful. In August 1909, Splash Dam No. 2, just under one mile above the first dam, was constructed, also another forty-acre lake. The No. 1 pond was longer than No. 2, but No. 2 was wider than No. 1. The Lewis firm also harvested ice at Beech Lake, a natural twenty-acre pond above Splash Dam No. 2. In January 1914, a post office was created for the community. The postal designation was Mountain Springs and thereafter the ice-cutting community at the two dams was known by its post office name.

Harvesting the Ice

In its simplest form, ice-cutting consisted of several phases of work. Snow was cleared off the surface of the lake to reach the ice. The ice field was then scored by horse or mule drawn ice plows in a pattern of large blocks called floats. Mechanical saws then cut nearly through the floats. Large sections of the ice field containing several floats were cut loose and pulled by men through an opened channel of water to a corner of the lake where the ice plant was located. There, the rafts of ice were broken into the floats which were nearly thirteen-feet square. The floats were pushed through a mill with a series of circular gang saws and cut nearly through every 32 inches. The floats were passed through a second set of gang saws which cut nearly through the strips every 22 inches. The floats were broken into connected strips of ice cakes and the strips broken again into individual 32 by 22-inch ice cakes. The ice cakes were picked up by a conveyor belt (gallery) which ran alongside a huge warehouse or ice plant. From the conveyor belt, the ice was loaded into railroad cars for immediate shipment, or into the warehouse for storage. From the warehouse the ice cakes could be unloaded all year around into railroad cars for shipment.

The details of ice-harvesting represent a fascinating glimpse into a once thriving industry which died a half-century ago. The ice-cutting season was generally in January, February, and March, and lasted only a few weeks, depending on weather and ice conditions. During the cutting season, 125 men would be employed cutting ice on the field, at the mills, on the gallery, and inside the rooms of the ice plant. It was seasonal work, providing employment for area farmers, laborers, and other workmen in the slow winter months. The men earned between 32 cents and 35 cents

The Mountain Springs ice plant at Splash Dam No. 1 is shown in a panoramic view. Unlike No. 2, the conveyor which lifted the ice into the plant was enclosed. The mill operations to cut the floats are in the center. A large tool house is shown at the far right.

an hour in the 1930s. Usually, a steady crew appeared each year for many seasons. After the ice-cutting season was over, only about twenty men were employed the remaining months to maintain the operations and to load railroad cars with ice from the plants.

In earlier days, there was not a road to Mountain Springs. The working men either walked to the site or took the train. But during the working season, many boarded at the few homes at Splash Dam No. 1 or they stayed at the boarding house there, perhaps only going home Saturday night and returning on Sunday or Monday morning. At times, too, railroad cars along sidings were converted into simple bunk houses. In the early 1920s, a dirt road was made up the mountainside from Route 118, which followed an older switch-back logging road which made travel to the site easier.

The workday was typically 7:00 a.m. to 5:30 p.m., with a half hour lunch break, but it could vary depending on circumstances. The men worked six days a week. If there was a short season due to poor ice conditions, the men would have to crowd the usual ten to twelve weeks of work into four to five weeks. There were no electric lights; sometimes night work occurred using lanterns.

Prior to the early 1930s, the Mountain Springs Ice Company first cut ice at Beech Lake, where there was not an ice plant. At Beech Lake, however, there would have been two sawing mills at the water's edge to cut blocks of ice into ice cakes, and a small conveyor system to load the cakes into railroad cars. Once Beech Lake was cut, the company moved to Splash Dam No. 1 to cut ice to load into railroad cars for shipment. Once the major consignment to the railroad company was met in two or three weeks, ice was cut at Dam No. 1 and at Dam No. 2 to fill the ice houses there. In a good season, 40,000 tons of ice were shipped from Beech Lake and Splash Dam No. 1 even before the two plants were filled. As many as 2,400 tons could be shipped out in railroad cars daily during the height of the cutting season. The ice house at Dam No. 1 was 300-feet long, 100-feet wide and 32-feet high. The ice house at Dam No. 2 was larger, 400-feet long, 150-feet wide, and 32-feet high. Plant No. 1 had six rooms, each nearly 50-feet wide and 100-feet long. Plant No. 2 had eight rooms nearly 50-feet wide and 150-

The ice plant at Splash Dam No. 2 is shown in mid-season. The lower conveyor is filled with ice cakes and the plant is nearly half full. The conveyor line runs in a counter-clockwise direction. At the far right is the boiler house which provided steam power for the conveyor. Up above is the "head-house" for the operator of the conveyor.

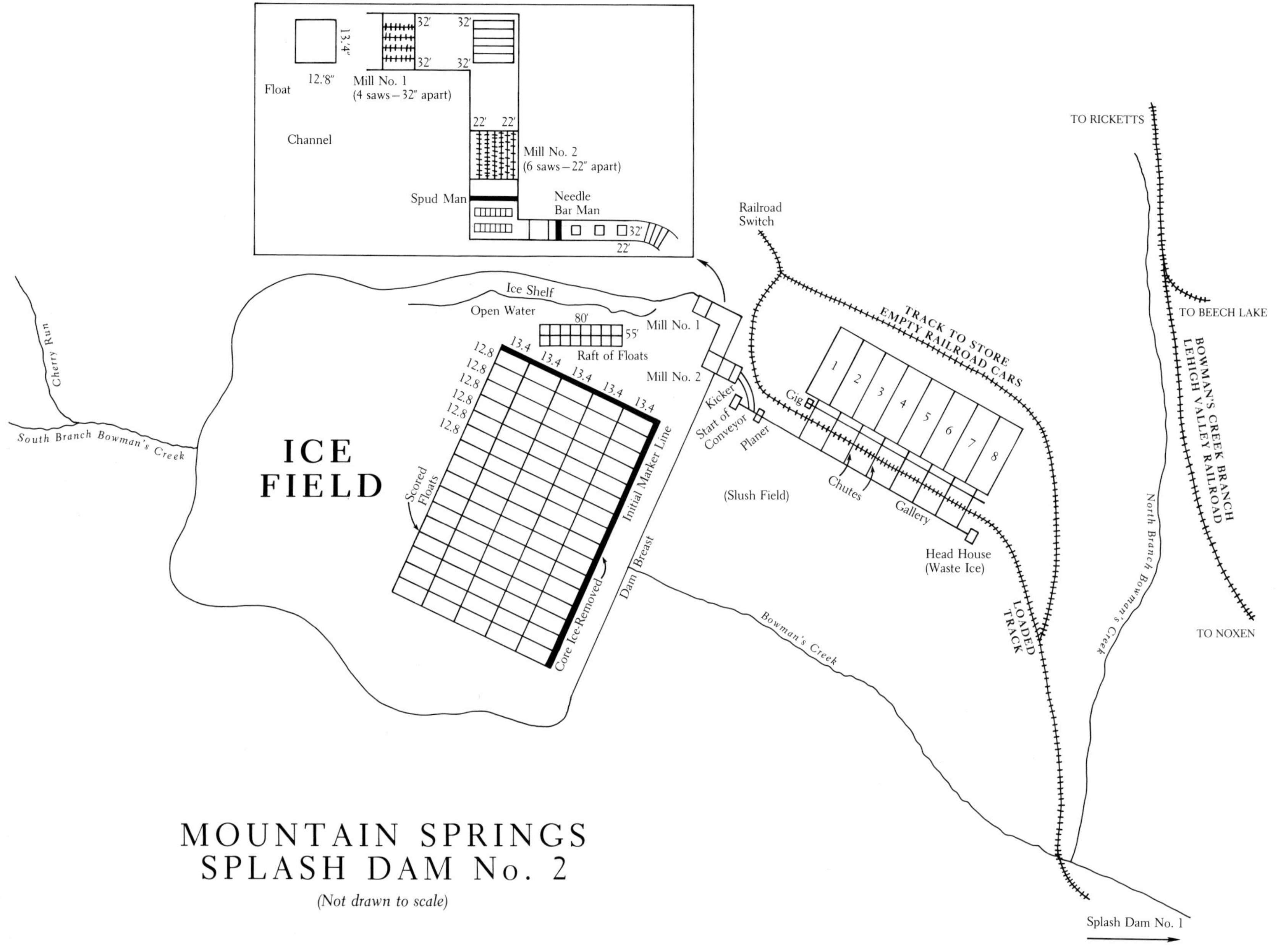

MOUNTAIN SPRINGS
SPLASH DAM No. 2

(Not drawn to scale)

Horse or mule teams pulling large scoops clear the snow cover from the ice. Once an initial marker line is drawn straight across the ice, a team scores the ice surface in a pattern 13.8 feet by 12.4 feet which are potential "floats" to be cut into ice cakes at the mills. Shown is the float marker which has two parallel rows of graduated sawing teeth.

feet long. All rooms were 32-feet high. Each plant had a storage capacity of 60,000 to 65,000 tons of ice.

The men dressed in whatever clothes they chose. Most always, however, on their feet they wore rubber arctic boots with triangular-shaped heel plates, tipped with metal points, like a cleat. Otherwise, the men wore long underwear, heavy coats, and wool trousers. Some wore overalls; others wore coveralls; many wore stocking caps. Frostbite was uncommon as men working on the ice and around the ice plant itself were active. Men slowly tugging rafts through the channel to the ice mills, however, had the coldest work, especially if the wind was driving and holding back the rafts from moving. The easiest work was probably in the "head house," an inside job where the conveyor was controlled. The switchers' work loading ice into railroad cars was cramped and difficult.

Ice ten-inches thick could be cut, but thirteen to fourteen inches was preferred. An ice auger was used to drill test holes. Ice thickness was measured with a gauge dropped through a hole drilled through the ice. The gauge had a hook at the end which would catch on the lip of the ice at the bottom of the hole. Harvesting was best when the temperature was 25 to 35 degrees. From 15 degrees to temperatures below zero, the ice was brittle and chipped or broke easily. In extremely cold weather, snow was left to accumulate on the ice to raise the temperature of the ice before the snow was cleared in sections and cut.

The ice along the shore had to bear the weight of the work animals, men, and equipment to reach the solid ice of the lake. If ice along the shoreline was thin, snow would be shoveled out fifteen feet from the shoreline. This snow cover slowed the natural freezing process along the shoreline and solid ice would form. If this trick failed, a wooden bridge to the thick ice beyond the shore was built. In the early years, horse-teams pulling scoops guided by a workman cleared the ice-covered lake of snow, which was shoveled off the lake and onto the shore. In later years, trucks with snow plows replaced the horse teams to clear snow. But the trucks were always two-wheel drive vehicles.

Work on the ice field began just above the dam. Using a plank board as a straight edge, and perhaps a nail keg as a sighting point, the workers scored the ice about one inch alongside the plank with a small marking saw—a plow-like saw with a handle to push it along. This process continued until a straight line was made across the lake roughly parallel to the dam. Once the initial line was cut, a field marker (a roughly square-metal frame with a series of graduated cutting teeth on each end) drawn by a team of horses or mules had one sawing end set into the initial marker line. The float marker was pulled along the marker line down the ice field which sawed the ice down nearly two inches deep in the marker line, while the opposite saw similarly scored the ice down at a parallel 13.4-foot interval. The process was continued up and down the field until a large field of ice had been scored in one direction with 13.4-foot parallel lines.

Another team starting with another marker line cross-scored the field at a right angle up the lake with another float marker, but at 12.8-foot intervals. The ice field eventually had a rectangular pattern of 13.4 by 12.8-foot scoring marks about two-inches deep. These scorings formed a series of quilt-like patterns on the ice field called floats; each float potentially held 35 cakes, each 32 by 22 inches when later cut from the float at the mills.

A gasoline driven rotary saw cut partly through the scorings of each 12.8 by 13.4 float. In earlier years horse or mule drawn iron ice plows were used for this work. On twelve-inch ice, the rotary plow cut down about eight or ten inches. Men with tamping bars would tamp ice chips around the floats where the corners met to prevent them from freezing solid again in the ice field.

In the next stage, a gasoline-powered saw called a grasshopper was used to make the final cut of the floats from the ice field.

Once the ice field is scored, the rotary plow, driven for many years by Jake Harris, cut down several inches along the scored ice.

But to move the initial floats to the mills at the head of the lake, sections of ice called "cores" had to be cut away at certain places, and a channel to the mills opened up. This excess core ice was pushed out of the way under the unused edges of ice. In time, a pond of open water to the dam and mills was created.

Once a large open-water area to the mills was open, 55 by 80-foot rafts containing several floats could be cut away by the grasshopper saw from the main ice field. Standing along the edge of the ice field and channel, men would pull the rafts away from the ice field and into the open water down to the mill. The men pulled or pushed ice rafts and floats with field hooks, long bars 14 to 16-feet long with a hook and a spike on the end. A horse, or later a truck, could be used to pull a float, but a skilled workman was best to prevent the raft or float corners from colliding with the rest of the ice field, breaking its corners, or getting caught under the ice field.

Once the ice was drawn near the mills, men using spudding bars would break away the 13.4 by 12.8-foot floats from each raft. A spud bar was a double-bladed (two-pronged) round bar about five-feet long. The larger rafts had already been plowed partly through by the rotary saw and they broke easily into the nearly thirteen-foot square floats.

The 13.4 by 12.8-foot float was initially passed through a mill where a series of four circular gang saws cut nearly through the float at 32-inch intervals. At the end of the first channel, the float passed at a right angle through a second mill where a series of six gang saws nearly cut through the float at 22-inch intervals. After passing through the second mill, a man on a plank over the channel with a spud bar could break off five strips of ice from the float. Each strip was 12.8-feet long and 32-inches wide and contained seven ice cakes.

The grasshopper saw cut away the initial floats from the ice to open up the field. At a later stage the grasshopper saw cut away large rafts of ice containing many floats. With the saw in this photograph is Leo Mincavage from Huntington Mills.

Two men are turning a raft of ice, which is scored across into several potential floats, while on the opposite side of the ice field another man is holding the other edge. The raft will be pivoted to permit the raft to be taken lengthwise down the water channel to the mill. The photograph was taken in late February 1940.

The strips of ice were picked up by a conveyor chain at the "kicker house." Before passing up the conveyor, a man with a needle bar spud off each individual 32 by 22-inch ice cake from the strip of ice. A needle bar was a five foot pole with a small blade at the end.

Although individual ice cakes were a uniform 32 by 22 inches, their thickness varied according to ice conditions on the lake. Typical thickness was 14 to 16 inches. Ten to twelve-inch ice occurred in a warm winter but was considered poor ice, but 17 to 18-inch ice could occur in severe winters, although it was very heavy and undesirable. Once the ice cakes were separated, they fell into individual buckets and up into the conveyor. They passed through an overhead planing mill which was a series of graduated knives which planed or scraped off the top of each cake to a uniform thickness. The cakes then passed under a heavy bristled brush which slightly scored or corrugated the top of the ice cakes which helped prevent their sticking together while in storage. There was a considerable amount of slush ice on the cakes from the planing and brushing process. Slush fell into a water-driven channel to the ground below. Two men continually worked to clear away the slush pile into a field.

The conveyor was powered by old belt-driven sawmill engines which burned soft coal in boilers. A flywheel and pulley arrangement connected the engines to the conveyor system. In the head house, forty feet above the boiler and engine room, the gallery operator engaged the conveyor with a simple clutch lever. He had a whistle to signal the men outside on the conveyor. Each of the chutes into the rooms had an electric bell to ring the head house if a problem occurred, one bell to stop the conveyor, two bells to restart the conveyor.

Eight men worked on the gallery at Plant No. 2 which they called the "hump." There was one man for each of the eight rooms

Two workmen pause for the photograph. With a pike pole, they can push a raft of ice down the channel to the mills and ice plant at Dam No. 2. As the rafts approach the mills, they are spudded apart into 13.8 by 12.4 foot floats.

in the ice house. At Plant No. 1, there were six rooms for six gallery men to service. Each man was responsible to push the ice cakes from the conveyor down a wooden chute into his assigned room. At Plant No. 2, for example, the first man took every eighth cake into the first room; the second man took every seventh cake; each man continued in turn down to the eighth room. At the end of the conveyor, any broken or unusable cakes passed up by the previous eight men fell to the ground. Broken cakes or cakes with broken corners could not be sold and were discarded. Broken corners left holes in the ice rooms and were treacherous to the men who worked there.

The chute from the gallery to the ice house had a slight downward pitch. The ice cakes from the gallery ran down a wooden chute to the ice house door. Near the door, the chute had a series of nails called scratchers driven upward through its bottom to catch and slow the cake's descent into the room. It was 150 feet from the door opening to the rear of the room.

In the beginning of the season, the gallery, which was manually raised and lowered by winches, was at the bottom of the ice house. The ice plant rooms were filled evenly during the conveying process. At the end of day, all eight rooms would usually have the same layers of ice. One layer or flat of ice in a room was about 1,070 cakes at Plant No. 2. The conveyor was winched upward as the rooms were filled during the season.

Inside the door to each of the eight rooms were two men called switchers who alternated in catching the ice cakes with switching hooks from the conveyor, shooting them across the ice floor to three other men who lined up the cakes inside the room until a full level of ice or flat was filled. The ice cakes were lined up in rows, filling the house from rear to front. A fourth "barman" separated the parallel rows of cakes with four inches of space to prevent their freezing into a solid mass. This process continued until all the rooms were filled. Originally, the filled ice house was topped with straw to insulate the ice, but straw made the cakes dirty. A black paper was later substituted for the straw to cover the top flat of ice.

For the balance of the year, when ice was not directly loaded from the lowered conveyor into railroad cars early in the season, the ice was unloaded from the filled ice houses, from the top downward, into railroad cars for shipment. Originally, the ice cakes were simply pushed down a wood chute to men inside the door of a railroad car for loading. But heavy cakes at times gained too much momentum and if not caught they could crash into, and sometimes through, the opposite side of the wooden railroad cars. A bucket-like machine called a gig was then devised to unload the ice. There was one gig to each ice house. The gig operated on a track which ran along the exterior of the ice house. It had a double chain and buckets which the gig operator could raise and lower above himself as the ice house was unloaded. Ice cakes were pushed from inside the room into the buckets which were lowered down to where the ice cakes fell into a wooden chute and then into the railroad cars.

Ice was usually loaded into 34 to 36-foot wooden, insulated railroad cars, which were originally built to haul potatoes, vegetables, and milk cans. But they had wooden end sills and underframing. When ice cars were hauled in long trains, they had a tendency to pull apart the sill and gearing at one end. If larger engines pushed against a train of these cars, the wooden underframing could also give way. When these filled cars were hauled on the main lines of the railroad system, the ice cars were usually at the end of the regular cars to minimize strain on them. If damage to the frame or sills still occurred, they had to be hauled behind the caboose. When the ice was removed, the damaged cars were refitted with steel underframes and gearing, or in later years the old cars were scrapped.

At No. 2 Dam, the first mill is at the right rear, the second mill is in the center, and the kicker house is at the left.

Plant No. 1 was usually unloaded before Plant No. 2. The men worked one room at a time beginning with room one. At the plants, there was a siding along the mountain where the railroad deposited empty cars. The men would open the railroad car brakes and a string of six to eight empties would descend by gravity to the plants. When filled they could be gravity-fed to the other side of the creek at Bean Run, where a locomotive would take them down the line.

Six men were used to unload a room. A bar man loosened the ice cakes. Two men with ice hooks moved the cakes and two others helped load it. A sixth man operated the gig. In a single day, one or two courses, or flats of ice, were unloaded from one room. In the railroad cars, there were two switchers to catch the ice and four placers in each car to place it properly from the ends of each car to the center.

Accidents at the ice-cutting plants were not as serious or common as in the adjoining lumbering operations, although work cutting ice with the sharp implements and saws caused cuts. From time to time, a man would fall through the ice and would be pulled out and sent to the boiler room to dry out. There were no known deaths or drownings among the men who worked on the ice or in the ice houses. Only two serious injuries are recalled. In January 1917, Russell Steele was hit on the head at the gallery by a falling piece of ice while he was climbing a ladder. He fell unconscious into the waste pile. He was taken by train to Wilkes-Barre General Hospital where he recovered consciousness four days later. Thirty years later, in February 1947, Albert Ferrey fell 32 feet from the gallery into a waste pile and broke his hip. He was taken by automobile to a Wilkes-Barre hospital.

Horse and mule teams did fall through the ice, and one team reportedly drowned in one of the lakes when they could not be unhitched in time. Each horse and mule had a choke rope around its neck. If an animal fell through the ice, the men first unhitched the animal from the ice plow or field marker. Planks were kept on

A float is emerging from the first mill at No. 1 Dam. Four circular saws have nearly cut through the float.

At the second mill at No. 1 Dam the workmen push the float against the right wall of the channel as the float passes under a series of six circular saws. Men in the background will spud off a strip of ice containing seven 32 by 22 inch cakes of ice.

the ice for these emergencies. A plank was slid under the chest of the animal who was pulled out by the ropes around him. The animal was covered with blankets and walked until he dried. The animals were not deterred after a fall, but would resume work on the ice. If equipment fell to the bottom of the lakes, which were only 15 to 20-feet deep, it could be retrieved.

Marketing the Ice

Seasonal variations affected the profits of the ice industry. A mild winter yielded a smaller harvest which would increase customer prices. Mild temperatures produced soft ice which could not be cut, or eight to ten-inch ice which was considered "thin" and subject to quicker melting in the transit and delivery phases of the business. The ice producer had to choose between cutting or waiting for a later freeze. There was a warm winter in 1912–1913, and the regional ice fields were only six to eight-inches deep. When a cold snap came in the first week of February, ice was quickly cut, with ten-inch ice at Mountain Springs and Lake Ganoga. Continuing winter snows also required additional labor costs to clear the ice fields, which could exceed the cost paid to cut the ice. This happened at Lake Ganoga in the early months of 1904. In the same cold winter, the ice was 16 to 24-inches thick, and while of good quality, it was very difficult to handle and added to the producers' costs.

The Lehigh Valley Railroad annually purchased hundreds of carloads of ice—perhaps 1,000 to 1,200 was average—for storage in railroad ice houses in Pennsylvania, New York, and New Jersey. Typically, an engine, several empty railroad cars, and a freight crew left the Lehigh Valley's Coxton Yards, above Pittston, early in the morning to arrive at Beech Lake or Mountain Springs when the

A strip of ice is pushed through the kicker to start through the conveyor process. Paul Maransky is the center man. Immediately after passing through the kicker another man with a needle bar will spike off individual cakes from the strips of ice.

employees started work at 7:30 a.m. A second train and crew could follow several hours later depending on the railroad's ice requirements.

Five engines were usually available during the ice loading season, with a couple laying over at Alderson where coal, fuel, and water were available. There was also a permanent standpipe to water engines at Beth Run, below Mountain Springs. The run to Mountain Springs from Alderson was single-track and operated on a "block system." Only one train could run in a block at a time; other traffic was sidelined and waited until clearance was received to operate on the track.

A couple of locomotives handled empty cars at train yards and assisted in assembling loaded cars into trains. At the end of the day, the extra engines were coupled to the last return train to Coxton. The entire operation was supervised by a railroad trainmaster to watch expenses because the cost of wages, particularly overtime, water, and fuel, could be substantial.

The return had relatively easy grade. Beech Lake has an elevation of 2,158 feet; Splash Dam No. 2, 1,853 feet; Splash Dam No. 1, 1,817 feet; and Harvey's Lake, 1,255 feet. There was a rise to Chesnut Ridge beyond the lake near Kunkle of 1,300 feet, after which the trains descended into the Wyoming Valley.

The railroads used immense quantities of ice in both passenger cars and, more importantly, in refrigerator cars carrying meats and perishables. These cars had four built-in bunkers for ice at the top of the car with a trap door for loading bunkers at the roof.

The Lehigh Valley Railroad shipped rail cars of ice to various storage stations along its line. In the early 1920s, for example, the Stull company supplied Wilkes-Barre, Coxton, Tunkhannock, and Sayre for the railroad. The Bear Creek Ice Company served the Lehigh Valley Railroad east of Wilkes-Barre at White Haven, Mauch Chunk, Mahoning, Hazleton, Easton, Phillipsburg, and

Jersey City. West of Sayre, the railroad had its own ice lake at Camden, New York, near Groton, on its Auburn rail line.

In addition to the Lehigh Valley Railroad, there was a substantial market for Mountain Springs ice in the Wyoming Valley. Individual ice dealers purchased carloads of ice along the Lehigh Valley's side tracks, and sometimes at private sidings, where dealers sold ice to retail and household customers directly from the rail car. Ice cars were usually open at 7:00 a.m. and the dealers had to sell the contents within 48 hours before the railroad moved the cars out again. If the dealer wanted to retain a car any longer, he paid the railroad an extra fee. But most dealers had small warehouses to store leftover ice so the rail cars could be released.

A mild winter producing a smaller ice crop would drive up retail prices; this happened in May 1913. A consumers' committee met with Arthur Stull at the Wilkes-Barre Chamber of Commerce offices to discuss the pricing situation, particularly since poor people were unable to readily afford ice and a distribution system of free ice appeared necessary.

Stull said his 1913 price to dealers was $2.80 per ton free-of-freight charges, compared to $1.40 in 1912 when ice was sold for 7 cents per hundred weight to dealers. Retailers in 1913 were selling it at 15 cents to heavy commercial users and it appeared there was a 100 percent mark-up. Ordinary customers and households paid more. But because of the mild winter, Stull explained he could only harvest 30,000 tons in 1913, compared to 60,000 tons in 1912. Only 8,000 tons were unsold in 1912 and were carried over into the 1913 season. The ice, too, was only 6.5 inches in 1913, compared to the usual 15 inches. Usually, the shrinkage rate was 10 to 20 percent, but the ice of 1913 would shrink 25 percent by the time it reached consumers' homes, a loss the dealers assumed in the natural course of business. The ice also easily broke and he lost 100 railroad cars of ice due to breakage and he discarded the ice. According to Stull, given the low harvest and high shrinkage,

A series of knives in the background will plane off the cake to a uniform thickness. The heavy brush will sweep off slush ice and give the top surface of each cake a rough finish.

the retailers' pricing structure would not produce for the retailers a profit in 1913 any different than the profit picture a year earlier. His own costs to harvest 30,000 tons in 1913 were the same costs he incurred in 1914 to harvest 60,000 tons, because he had to install a temporary electrical lighting system at his plants to get whatever harvest he could at night the first week of February, a very late season.

At least in the earlier years, ice dealers minimized their business problems by annually combining to fix wholesale prices to retail dealers, partly to deflect local competition among the local producers, and perhaps partly to protect against in-roads by the huge national ice company combinations, like the American Ice Company who controlled major mid-Atlantic markets. The major producers in the region were the Pocono Ice Company, Bear Creek Ice Company, and Arthur Stull's Mountain Springs Company. But occasionally a price war did erupt among the local producers, as happened from mid-April to May 15, 1915. Prices in 1914 were 25 cents per hundred weight to heavy customers, 30 cents to ordinary business customers, and 40 cents for family users. The Pocono company, however, cut heavy users' costs to 15 cents. The Pocono firm had been a buyer of ice from Arthur Stull, but recently it opened its own ice field at a pond near Nuangola, near present-day Mountaintop, in the Wyoming Valley, and it planned to cut into Stull's retail market in the valley. But Stull supplied ice to five major valley retail companies and he cut his prices, too. Shortly, price cuts across the board were in place at 15, 20, and 25 cents, which delighted the ordinary homeowner, but were ruining the ice dealers. Companies not affiliated with the Pocono firm or Stull—Heart Lake, Ganoga Lake, Peoples Ice, Spring Lake, and Mountain Lake—were trapped in the war and struggled to maintain competitive prices. Finally, on May 14, 1915, the companies again combined to set a uniform scale of 20, 25, and 35 cents—five cents below 1914 prices for the three levels of customers which

A row of ice cakes are fed by the conveyor into the eight rooms of Plant No. 2. The plant is nearly full as the chutes are nearly to the top of the rooms of the plant on the left.

Shown is a closeup of the "hump" late in the season with one man visible in the center to push cakes into a room. Apparently, the other rooms are filled. Otherwise, there would be a man on each chute loading each of the eight rooms. Here, only a middle and end room are being filled.

settled the local market. To discourage the purchase of smaller pieces, less than one hundred pounds, common in many homes, which was unprofitable to retail dealers, the price was raised to 50 cents per hundred weight, or five cents for a ten-pound piece.

There were also individual delivery men who purchased ice daily from a dealer and operated their own horse-teams and wagons, delivering ice throughout the valley. Households had a square card marked "none" on one corner, with each of three other corners marked with a common ice size and current price. The card was placed in a window with the desired corner top-most to tell the traveling "ice-man" if the household wanted ice and the size block. The ice-man had a scale in the wagon, chopped off a block and carried it with tongs to the house. Young boys liked to follow the ice-wagon in the summer to salvage the dropped ice scraps.

There were a variety of ice-boxes for home use. The least expensive was a double chest with insulated double-layers of wood. The top chest was a sheet metal box with a hinged double-wood top and the ice was dumped inside it. The bottom chest was also sheet metal lined; it contained shelves and had a hinged door. The melting ice cooled the metal lining which kept food cold. The melting ice drained to a pan underneath the ice chest, or through a pipe to the outside of the house.

Other important commercial users of ice included meat processing and packing plants—conveniently located along railroad lines in downtown Wilkes-Barre—large stores, hotels, and restaurants. They had walk-in cooling rooms where ice was placed on racks.

In February 1933, Arthur L. Stull formed Arthur L. Stull and Company, a partnership to operate the Mountain Springs Ice Company. He transferred a one-eighth interest in the lands to his son, Robert A. Stull (1895–1980), and a two-eighths interest to his brother, Albert A. Stull. These two transferred their interests to the new company, as did Arthur L. Stull with his five-eighths

For a short time Glenn Kitchen tried a rotary saw, used at Pocono Lake, to cut rafts and floats at Mountain Springs, but it was not as useful as the traditional rotary plow.

interest. The lands and ice interests transferred to the new company were the interests Arthur L. Stull obtained when he broke with Albert Lewis in 1912.

The Village of Mountain Springs

There was a small village at Plant No. 1 with a few homes, boarding house, and school. The foreman and long-term laborers lived in the village. Noah McCloskey was the earliest foreman. He was born in Lehigh Tannery and previously worked at Bear Creek and Stull. Noah's wife, Emma McCloskey, became the first postmistress at Mountain Springs on January 20, 1914. Her daughter, Emily McCloskey Kitchen, married Art Kitchen, who began working at Mountain Springs after World War I. Emily McCloskey Kitchen became the postmistress in 1929.

Noah McCloskey was followed by Harry Majors and Joe Maransky as foreman at the ice plants. Finally, Art Kitchen was the last foreman under White and Davis from the early 1940s until the plants closed.

On the hill above the ice dam, Art Kitchen had his home. The Kitchen home kept candy, tobacco, and a few supplies for sale. A company store was not available, and the train was the source of food and other supplies. In the next home lived Paul Maransky, the field foreman and "bar man" in the plant rooms in the summer. His three sons also worked at Mountain Springs. There was also the two-story boarding house which could serve 75 to 100 men. A couple or family was hired by the ice company to operate it. A third house was generally associated with John Micklo, who had many children. There was also a barn where the horses and mules were kept during the ice-cutting season. They were brought on the train from the Stull farm in Alderson.

At the bottom of the hill nearer the dam, there were three other homes, which, in the 1930s, were occupied by John Yellitz, Mike Markovitz, and John Pocono. They, too, had families, and

The Mountain Springs boarding house was located at Splash Dam No. 1.

their sons usually also worked on the ice. The homes also kept boarders. For example, Rube Downing worked season after season on the ice and stayed with the Kitchen family. He formerly worked at Ricketts. George "Tonto" Belicci regularly boarded with Markovicz.

The community was small because less than two dozen people were employed on a year-round basis. Nevertheless, there was also a one-room school which taught grades one through eight. The first school was at Bean Run. The Mountain Springs school followed the Bean Run school. Teachers at these schools were Delbert Hines, Velma Kocher Whitesell, Maria Harrison, Winifred Holmes, Andrew Keller, Mary McCloskey Driesbach, and Celia Hortop O'Leary. At the end, the Mountain Springs school only had three pupils: Mary Louise Buckalew, Marian Maransky, and Robert H. Lasko. When Mary Louis Buckalew completed eighth grade in 1938, the school was closed, and the other two pupils were transferred to Mooretown.

When ice-cutting ceased, only Art and Emily Kitchen stayed in the town. Art Kitchen traveled down the mountain to meet the mail carrier three times each week on Route 118. Mountain Springs, with a population of two people, was considered the second smallest post office in the United States. Needles, California, had a population of one. When the post office at Mountain Springs closed on January 20, 1953, Art and Emily Kitchen moved to Pleasant Hill.

Decline and End

By the late 1930s, the ice industry was in decline. In May 1937, the Bear Creek Ice Company only stored 76,000 tons of ice. Ten years earlier the harvest was nearly five times greater. Similarly, the Pocono Lake ice plant only stored 46,000 tons. The last ice was cut at Bear Creek in 1938, after which the Lehigh Valley Railroad removed the tracks to the company plants.

During the winter of 1935–1936, the first two or three rooms in the old Ice Plant No. 1 at Mountain Springs collapsed after heavy

The Mountain Springs school house closed in 1938.

snows. The plant was not used for storage any longer, but was used to load railroad cars. One or two rooms at Ice Plant No. 2 collapsed during the early 1940s, but loading continued in the other rooms during the ice-cutting season.

In April 1942, Arthur L. Stull died, followed by his brother Albert A. Stull in September 1946. In August 1945, the estate of Arthur L. Stull, along with Albert A. Stull and Robert A. Stull, sold the Mountain Springs Ice Company lands to Ralph A. Davis, who, in December 1945, joined with John W. White in a partnership to continue the ice business.

Passenger service on the Bowman's Creek railroad ended in 1936, except for special excursions to Harvey's Lake. The Lehigh Valley Railroad sought the abandonment of freight service on the Bowman's Creek line in 1938, but the Interstate Commerce Commission denied the application. The ice trains and the Noxen tannery were its only significant freight. In late January 1942, for example, forty cars of ice were shipped daily over the line from Mountain Springs. But such shipments lasted only a couple of weeks in the ice-cutting season. During the balance of the year, only a few ice cars were shipped weekly from the ice plants. Undoubtedly, the line was very unprofitable to the railroad.

In late 1948, the Lehigh Valley Railroad closed traffic above Noxen on the Bowman's Creek Branch. The ice industry was dying and provided too little traffic on the railroad. Mechanical refrigeration techniques readily produced artificial ice for industry. The railroads were increasingly using dry ice or mechanically refrigerated cars. After World War II, homeowners routinely were using refrigerators and freezers. The public, too, no longer had to contend with periodic fears regarding the safety of natural ice. With the loss of the railroad in 1948, the ice industry in Mountain Springs closed after the 1948 season. Plant No. 2 was destroyed by a fire in the summer of 1948.

KETTS' BATTERY
1st PENNA
RTILLERY, PENNA RESERVE CORPS
2418. CEMETERY HILL.

Col. Robert Bruce Ricketts (1839-1918)

My command at Gettysburg [on July 2, 1863] consisted of Batteries "F & G" First Pennsylvania Light Artillery—Battery "G" having been attached to my original command, Battery "F," a few weeks before the battle—the two organizations forming one full six gun Battery.

We were attached to the Artillery Reserve, Army of the Potomac, and marched with that command on the morning of July 2d from Taneytown to Gettysburg arriving on the field about noon.

At 4:00 p.m. I was ordered by Captain Huntington, to whose Brigade of the Artillery Reserve my Battery was attached, to report to Colonel C.S. Wainwright, who commanded the line of Artillery on East Cemetery Hill. We moved up the Taneytown road by Gen. Meade's Headquarters, halted for a short time behind Cemetery Hill, and then moved up the Baltimore Pike and relieved Cooper's Battery, "B" 1st Penna. Light Artillery, on East Cemetery Hill.

My position was in front of where the observatory now stands with my left [artillery] piece near the stone wall—on my left over the stone wall was Wiednick's New York Battery with, I believe, six guns; on my right, down the hill was Reynold's "L," 1st New York Battery with, I think, six guns. All of the above three Batteries, Wiednicks, Reynolds and mine had, as I remember it, 10 pounder regulation rifled guns. Behind my Battery was Stewart's Battery, "B" 4th U.S. Artillery, with four 12 pounder smooth-bore guns—two of his guns were on the Baltimore Pike facing the town and two were in rear of the two right guns of my battery facing to our front.

After going into position we were engaged with the enemy's artillery during the afternoon until Johnson's [Confederate] Division formed on Benner's Hill for the attack on Culp's Hill. We opened on them as soon as they appeared on the hill and continued the fire as they advanced down the hill to Rock Creek and into the woods at the foot of Culp's Hill. When they got into the woods between Rock Creek and Culp's Hill, our fire was guided by the smoke of [their] musketry fire rising above the trees.

At about dusk, and while we were still firing on Johnson's troops—Early's Division [the Louisiana Tigers]—which had formed in a depression running from the town to Rock Creek—suddenly appeared in our front and with the "rebel yell" charged directly on East Cemetery Hill. They were at once under the fire of Wiednick's, Reynolds' and my Battery from East Cemetery Hill and of Steven's Maine Battery on Culp's Hill which had an enfilading fire on them. As far

Col. R. Bruce Ricketts, second from left, stands beside the Ricketts Battery monument on East Cemetery Hill, site of Ricketts' heroic defense at Gettysburg on July 2, 1863. His son, William R. Ricketts, is sitting on the ground, fourth from left, in this circa 1893 photograph.

as my Battery was concerned, we opened at once with double-shotted canister and although it was the dusk of the evening and the smoke of the guns made it quite dark, I do not think that any of the enemy who charged in our immediate front were able to reach our guns. Our infantry were, however, driven back through the Batteries and Wiednick's Battery was compelled to [retreat]. The left flank of my Battery was then completely exposed and the enemy who had climbed the hill in front of Wiednick's Battery were able to reach the stone wall on the left of my Battery. They fired directly down the line of the guns, but fortunately they could not see in the darkness that the ground fell away from my left piece toward the right of the Battery. I remember well the roar of the torrent of bullets as they passed over our heads.

My men behaved splendidly in this great emergency. Soon after I went into position, Colonel Wainwright said to me, "If a charge is made on this point you will not limber up and escape under my circumstances, but fight your Battery as long as you can." I repeated this order to my officers and men, and I do not remember ever to have heard of any member of my command having failed to do his whole duty. Only once, for a moment, when the Infantry were falling back through the Battery, some of my men gave back, but were instantly rallied with the cry "Die on your own soil boys before you give up your guns."

Some of the enemy crossed the stone wall and there was hand to hand fighting in the left of the Battery reaching as far as the 3d Gun from the left, my men fighting with handspikes, hammer stones and pistols. I devoted my energies to keeping up the fire from as many guns as we could and in going along the guns I suddenly came upon a group, just in rear of the 3d Gun from the left. The group consisted of Lieut. C.B. Brockway, acting Sergeant Stratford, and a confederate soldier who was on the ground. Stratford had a musket [held as a club] which was on the point of falling [on the Confederate] when I seized it and probably saved the poor fellow's life. I do not, however, remember now what became of him. The story as told by Brockway afterwards was that the confederate demanded Stratford's surrender when Brockway, who was near and forgetting he had a sword, picked up a stone and struck him on the head. Stratford seized the man's musket and fired wounding him severely and then clubbed the musket and would no doubt have brained him if I had not caught the gun at that moment. At about this time and near the same place, James H. Riggin, the Guidon bearer [our flag], staggered against me and fell with the cry "help me Captain." When we found him after the fight he was dead and the sleeve of the right arm of my coat was covered with the brave fellow's blood. We afterward learned that in a personal encounter with a Confederate officer who had attempted to capture the Battery Guidon—which was planted near the Second Gun from the left—[Riggin] had shot the officer with his revolver, but at the same moment the staff of the Guidon was shot in two and poor Riggin was shot through the body.

Three of my men, Francis Reid, Oscar G. Lanaber and John M. Given, commoners on the left piece, were carried away as prisoners. [Given was wounded and died in the hands of the enemy. The other two were afterwards exchanged.] The situation had now become really desperate—Stewart with his two 12 pounder guns on the Pike was firing canister, sweeping the ground that had been occupied by Wiedrick's Battery. There was nothing left on East Cemetery Hill to resist the onslaught of the enemy but the hand-full of brave men of my Battery—but even with the favoring circumstances of the dusk of the evening, the smoke of the guns and the lay of ground, they were becoming exhausted and would soon have been overcome—but just at this time—probably the most critical moment during the Battle of Gettysburg—Carroll's Brigade of the 2d Army Corps, sent in on the run by Genl. Hancock, arrived and passing by the right of my Battery and down the hill opened fire and the enemy retired.

I never knew how long the fight lasted on the evening of the 2nd, but I remember that after everything had become quiet the full moon was just above Culp's Hill.

R. Bruce Ricketts
September 10, 1893

The Ricketts Family

On East Cemetery Hill the early evening of July 2, 1863, the Ricketts legend was born. Had the famed and feared Louisiana Tigers broken through Ricketts' Battery to split apart the Union Army, the Confederates may have won at Gettysburg. The Tigers

The only known photograph of Robert Bruce Ricketts in Civil War uniform was taken at the McClees studio in Philadelphia probably in December 1863, five months after the Gettysburg battle.

had never lost a battle charge before Ricketts Battery and Carroll's Brigade had repelled them. The Tigers lost nearly 1,200 of their 1,500 men in the charge against Ricketts' Battery, but Ricketts Battery lost only seven men, with another 23 wounded. After Gettysburg the Tigers were never reformed as a military unit.

The young captain, R. Bruce Ricketts, who defended East Cemetery Hill t.ıe fateful July day at Gettysburg, had set aside a promising career in law to join the Union Army. He had a brother, Col. William Wallace Ricketts, who attended West Point. But he died at age 26 at home a year earlier in August 1862 after resigning from the service due to ill health. Their grandfather, Lieutenant Edward Ricketts, was a Revolutionary Army officer in the Pennsylvania militia.

The original Ricketts settlers in our region were the brothers Elijah G. Ricketts (1803–1877) and Clemuel Ricketts (1794–1858), who relocated from Fairfield County, Ohio, in 1822, to Orangeville in Columbia County. The settlement was named after Orange County, New York, and Orange, New Jersey, the home of other settlers in the village.

Elijah Ricketts, a general merchant and farmer, married Margaret Leigh Lockart (1810–1891) in 1830, building a home which still stands on the corner of Main and Ricketts Street in Orangeville. Of Scot-

Col. William Wallace Ricketts posed for an ambrotype in his Civil War uniform but died at home in Orangeville in 1862. He is buried in the Ricketts plot at the Laurel Hill Cemetery in Orangeville, Columbia County.

tish and English descent, Col. Robert Bruce Ricketts was the fifth son of nine children of this union.

Elijah Ricketts and his brother Clemuel Ricketts were huntsmen, and each spring and fall they usually stayed at Schrifogel's Hotel on the Loyalsock Creek, two miles west of Lopez. Family tradition holds that the two brothers found the hotel full one fall day in 1850, and they spent an uncomfortable night on the parlor floor, after which they decided to build their own sporting lodge. They purchased nearly 5,000 acres of land, including Long Pond (Ganoga Lake), and constructed the Stone House near the lake in 1852. The three-story Stone House, built of field limestone, is of Colonial design and is now maintained by the Ganoga Lake Association. During the 1850s, the Stone House served as a lodge and tavern which some called "Ricketts' Folley" due to its wilderness isolation.

The Stone House was reached by a stage line (1827–1851) on the Susquehanna and Tioga Turnpike (1822–1907). The turnpike was a crude road from Berwick to Tioga Point, near Athens, in Bradford County, and then on to Elmira, New York. In earlier days thousands of lumber rafts annually descended the Susquehanna River from Elmira, New York, and Pennsylvania's northern counties, to lumber markets in Harrisburg, and the turnpike through Sullivan County was a short-cut for the raftsmen to return home. The old road generally parallels Route 487 for a portion of the Red Rock area. The stage line left Berwick in the morning stopping at noon at the Long Pond Tavern, which pre-dated Ricketts' Stone House, and guests stayed overnight at Schrifogel's Hotel, eight miles away on Loyalsock Creek. This stretch was called "the road to hell." The turnpike was a county road from 1852 to 1907, when present Route 487 was constructed.

At the outbreak of the Civil War in the spring of 1861, R. Bruce Ricketts had only recently graduated from Wyoming Seminary. He was planning to attend Yale to become a lawyer. Instead, he enlisted as a private in Battery F of the 1st Pennsylvania Light Artillery (the 43rd Regiment, Pennsylvania Volunteers). Mustered into service on July 8, 1861, Ricketts was promoted a month later to First Lieutenant. The regiment was armed at Washington, D.C., but never served as a unified command. Battery F was assigned in September 1861 to the 5th Corps of the Army of the Potomac and came under fire for the first time in mid-December 1861 against Confederate troops on the upper Potomac River. By February 1863, Ricketts commanded Battery F, but he was now attached to the 2nd Division of the 1st Corps. In May 1863, Ricketts was promoted to Captain, and Battery G of the 1st Pennsylvania Artillery was also attached to his command. Battery F and Battery G were called Ricketts' Battery during the course of his command.

In December 1864, Ricketts was promoted to Major and left his famous battery to command Second Corps batteries attached to the North Corps line in Petersburg, Virginia. He subsequently served as Inspector and later Chief of Artillery for the Ninth Corps. In March 1865, one month before Lee's surrender on April 9, 1865, Ricketts was named a Colonel, last serving as Inspector of the Artillery Reserve, which was nearly all of the artillery in the Union army. He was honorably discharged on June 3, 1865. During the war, he served in several of the most famous battles of the war including Second Bull Run, Antietam, Fredericksburg, Chancel-

lorsville, and the Wilderness Campaign. His troops were in 56 battles and engagements, and were under fire 131 times during the war, but Ricketts was never wounded.

Ricketts returned to Wilkes-Barre after the war but never resumed his law studies. On October 1, 1868, he married Elizabeth Reynolds (1842–1918), descendant of a pioneer Wyoming Valley family. Her father, William C. Reynolds, was in the coal and banking business. Ricketts decided to speculate in the wild lands of North Mountain. His uncle, Clemuel Ricketts, died in March 1858 and his father, Elijah, acquired Clemuel's interests at Lake Ganoga. In September 1869, the 30-year-old R. Bruce Ricketts purchased from his father Long Pond, the Stone House, and nearly 1,700 surrounding acres in Sullivan County. He subsequently acquired the balance of the family lands, another 3,000 acres.

In the early 1880s, Col. Ricketts acquired a high Victorian Gothic double-block mansion at 80–84 South River Street in Wilkes-Barre. The historic street fronting the river common lands was the site of several homes constructed by Wilkes-Barre's coal and financial leaders. The Ricketts mansion was originally built in the 1860s by George Murray Reynolds (1838–1904), oldest brother of the Colonel's wife. It later became a double-block and was shared by Benjamin Reynolds (1840–1913), the youngest brother of the Colonel's wife. Benjamin Reynolds was primarily associated with the Anthracite Savings Bank, which merged in 1912 with the Miners National Bank (now the United Penn Bank).

The R. Bruce Ricketts and Benjamin Reynolds double-block home is shown at 80–82 South River Street in Wilkes-Barre. In 1990 it became a Wilkes University dormitory. It is now painted ivory; the fencing was removed long ago, along with the porch entrance on the right side of the building.

The Lake Ganoga Estate

The Ricketts' lands at Lake Ganoga were the subject of several interesting historical events apart from the lumbering era which began in the early 1890s.

In the years 1872–1875, Ricketts maintained a partnership with a Mr. William Curtin of Philadelphia and a Col. Wilson of Trenton, New Jersey, in the lumber business. They had a mill half a mile southeast of the Stone House. Lumber from the mill was used to construct a three-story addition to the Stone House hotel. The addition was familiarly known as the "Ark." Begun in 1872, it opened in the summer of 1873. The Ricketts estate with its new addition was called the North Mountain House. Open all year, the hotel catered to an ever-growing social network of Ricketts' relations and friends until 1903, when the hotel was closed and the Stone House became the summer residence of Col. Ricketts and his wife. The ark was torn down in 1897 and the site became a garden.

The earliest American summer school was begun by Col. Ricketts at the North Mountain House in the summer of 1873. There were two small-frame buildings surrounded by tents to serve 26 students. The instructors were Dr. Joseph Rothrock, Dr.

John H. Green was a slave attached to a Confederate officer during the Civil War. During the great battle of July 3, 1863, known as Pickett's Charge, Green was separated from the Confederates and was captured by the Union Army. He was placed in charge of Col. R. Bruce Ricketts whose own valet was killed in the war. Green stayed with the Ricketts family until his death in 1923. Green was a tremendous reader of history, science, and poetry, a music collector, and radio enthusiast. The Colonel provided Green an education for the ministry and John Green subsequently ministered at Ganoga. A master cook, conversationalist, and philosopher, he was well-loved at the Lake Ganoga community. He was treated as a member of the Ricketts family, handled estate affairs and the Ganoga ice-company, and was buried in the Ricketts' family plot at Ganoga.

Howard Kelley, Dr. Lewis Taylor, and the artist Eugene Frank. Dr. Rothrock later became a national conservation figure and the "Father of Pennsylvania Forestry."

The principal attractions at the Ricketts estate were Lake Ganoga and the waterfalls along Kitchen Creek. Lake Ganoga was originally called Robinson's Lake, named after a hunter who had a cabin at the upper end of the lake in the early 1800s. But it generally was called Long Pond because of its shape. It is nearly one mile long, 700 to 800 feet wide, covers about 70 acres, and is fed by underground springs and a small spring inlet. In 1881, State Senator Charles R. Buckalew of Bloomsburg suggested to Col. Ricketts the name "Ganoga," a Senaca Indian word meaning "water on the mountain." At 2,266 feet above tide level, it is the highest lake east of the Rocky Mountains.

The falls along the east and west branches of Kitchen's Creek were discovered in 1865 by two fishermen who were staying at the Stone House. In 1889, a crew of six men, led by Matt Hirlinger, were hired to construct the trail and stone steps around the falls. The difficult work was not completed until 1893. The 21 falls along Kitchen's Creek were named by Col. Ricketts. Several have native American designations, but others were named after Ricketts' friends, relations, or other associations with his North Mountain retreat.

Colonel Ricketts also constructed a forty-foot observation tower at Grand View, a peak near the Stone House from which guests could see twenty miles into the mountains. Today the state Forest Department has an eighty-foot steel fire observation tower at the site, and from it a view into eleven counties and three states can be seen on a clear day.

The North Mountain Fishing Club was formed in 1879 and continued until the hotel closed in 1903. Hotel guests paid a one dollar fee to fish Kitchen Creek. But before 1893, there was no path along the falls. The North Mountain Club was reformed in 1907 and purchased a tract of land on Spring Brook, a branch of Loyalsock Creek, three miles north of the Stone House, but did not utilize this land. In May 1909, the club leased Kitchen's Creek and certain lands for hunting and fishing. The clubhouse was initially a renovated Trexler and Turrell lumber camp house at Lake Rose, but later the club purchased and renovated a clubhouse it still uses at the foot of Red Rock Mountain.

Ricketts As Land Speculator

During the 1870s and 1880s, Ricketts purchased additional lands, often through tax sales in Luzerne, Wyoming, and Sullivan counties. He was aided by close business and legal associates including Michael Meylert, another Sullivan County land baron, and E. P. Darling, a Wilkes-Barre lawyer.

Edward Peyson Darling (1831–1889) was a graduate of Amherst College and was admitted to law practice in Reading in 1853. He moved to Wilkes-Barre in 1855 and had local banking, utility and railroad interests, in addition to serving as trustee of several local charities. He assisted Col. Ricketts with his land acquisition and served as his legal confidant in the resolution of financial and legal issues surrounding Ricketts' land speculation.

Michael Meylert (1823–1883) was the son of Secku Meylert (1784–1849), a native of Germany who served in Napoleon's army and who immigrated to Sullivan County. By 1845, the elder Meylert, in partnership with others, purchased 33,000 acres in four counties. His son, Michael Meylert, became a surveyor and engineer who, at age 26, inherited his father's interest in the vast unbroken lands.

Meylert, like Ricketts, needed a railroad to exploit his land holdings. As early as 1851, Meylert planned railroad ventures for the region which were either unsuccessful for lack of sufficient capital, or had a fitful history, until many years later when the Sullivan and State Line Railroad and the Williamsport and North Branch Railroad were constructed, both of which can historically be traced to Meylert's efforts.

Until his death in 1883, Meylert was in league with Ricketts

in the acquisition of North Mountain tracts through tax sales. These cheaply purchased lands, however, presented Ricketts with very thorny questions of inaccurate surveys, conflicting titles, squatters and timber thieves. Ricketts had to continually engage surveyors and lawyers to obtain clear titles to his lands. Ricketts also employed timber guards to protect his lands since they were constantly subjected to bark and timber stealing. These thieves, however, were extremely difficult to prosecute. As a concession to the difficulty of determining ownership to the state's wild lands, a defendant could escape conviction if he swore in court he did not know he was trespassing on another person's property. The available evidence indicates Ricketts usually was not successful in removing timber thieves from his property until the early 1890s when he leased his lands to a major lumber firm.

Ricketts, Meylert, and Darling sought to exploit their land ventures as early as March 1871 when they formed the Mehoopany Mining and Manufacturing Company to mine semi-anthracite coal and to timber 14,000 acres, owned by Ricketts, in Forkston Township in Wyoming County and in Colley Township in Sullivan County. In January 1872, Ricketts reputedly sold the 14,000 tract to the company for $200,000, but it is likely he received stock in lieu of cash for the transaction. Ricketts was not the full owner of the tract. He was in debt to his business and legal associates who helped him acquire his properties and they held certain ownership interests in the lands. The deed to the sale was not recorded until 21 years later when the company and the various ownership interests or their heirs sold the tract to a tanning syndicate as part of the Jennings Brothers lumbering operation in Lopez. For two decades after formation of the Mehoopany Mining and Manufacturing Company, a railroad was not available to haul timber, and the company was limited to small operations along the tracts' creeks, principally the Mehoopany Creek, and presumably to the mill town of Mehoopany, Pennsylvania, on the Susquehanna River.

To the right is the Ricketts Stone House. To the left is the "ark," the frame hotel which was dismantled in 1897. A stone addition was added to the main house in 1913.

By 1886, Ricketts still owned 45,000 acres of undeveloped timberland in Sullivan and Wyoming counties. This figure includes the 14,000 acres supporting the Mehoopany Mining and Manufacturing Company. His only substantial sale had been an additional 13,000 acres he had sold to Albert Lewis's Lehigh Valley Railroad venture in 1876.

His mortgage debt on the 45,000 remaining acres was heavy. Ironically, the railroad industry alone had a vast market for timber to make ties, trestles, and rolling stock. The mining industry, too, had a vast need for lumber. In an inflated evaluation to attract investors, it was estimated that Ricketts' lands were worth nearly $6 million if a railroad were built through them.

A number of New York, Philadelphia, and Boston lumber merchants were interested in the Ricketts lands, but their propositions were not ambitious enough. Ricketts had hoped to sell all of his lands, with the exception of the Lake Ganoga estate, in a massive deal which would make him wealthy and curtail the management of his troublesome land empire.

In the summer of 1886, the state political conventions met to nominate candidates for state offices. For state governor, which then was a two-year term, they nominated Gen. James A. Beaver, and William T. Davies for lieutenant-governor. The Democrats were bitterly divided into three factions. The regular party nominated Chauncey F. Black for governor and Col. R. Bruce Ricketts as lieutenant-governor. The Ricketts nomination sought to take advantage of his Civil War record, which may have been an awkward decision. It was nearly impossible to persuade Ricketts to talk about his personal accomplishments or his Civil War fame. During this period in the state's history, the Republican party firmly controlled state politics. The Democrats lost the governor's race and the two houses of the state general assembly by a wide plurality. The Ricketts nomination did carry Luzerne County for the Democrats in the governor's race. Within a couple of weeks after the election, an offer was made to Ricketts which captivated him for the next four years.

The English Deal

In November 1886, an incredibly welcome plan was proposed to Ricketts. In Columbia County, the thirty-mile Bloomsburg and Sullivan Railroad was under construction from the junction of the Delaware, Lackawanna, and Western Railroad at Bloomsburg, on the Susquehanna River, to Jamison City, the head of a new lumbering district on the northeast corner of the Columbia–Sullivan County line. The town was named after B.K. Jamison, a Philadelphia banker who was financing the railroad and the Jamison City lumbering development. Jamison City was only a few miles south from the Ricketts estate. At this time, a syndicate, composed of Pennsylvania banking and political interests, including A.G. Curtin and H.M. Hoyt, former governors of Pennsylvania, wanted 15,000 acres of lands in lower Sullivan County adjacent to Ricketts' tracts to harvest for the mill at Jamison City.

In May 1888, B.K. Jamison, Morton McMichael, and H.C. Gibson, all Philadelphia investors, secured the option for 15,000 acres of Sullivan County lands, drained by Fishing Creek, to feed the Jamison City operation with lumber. They, in turn, contracted with Col. James Corcoran of Williamsport to operate the mill at Jamison City. The lands purchased in 1889 included 10,000 acres, known as the Tinsman and Wolverton tracts, and half of the Craig and Blanchard tracts, another 4,278 acres, all of which were in Davidson Township. They were owned by a few estates and individuals, but Col. Ricketts was not one of the owners. The syndicate formed the North Mountain Lumber Company to control the tracts.

Of course, a railroad to the Jamison syndicate lands could also benefit Ricketts' adjacent 45,000 acres, and Jamison drew Ricketts into the plan. Ricketts and the Jamison City investors negotiated to extend the Bloomsburg and Sullivan Railroad through Sullivan County to Ricketts' lands. Then the plan envisioned the creation of the Central Pennsylvania Railway, Land and Timber Company, Ltd., which was to be formed in England. The English corporation was composed primarily of Philadelphia and London banking and lumber interests, some of whom were also members of the Jamison City syndicate. The corporation planned to purchase the controlling interest of the Bloomsburg and Sullivan Railroad Company and to combine the 15,000 acres of the Jamison syndicate with the purchase of Ricketts' 45,000 North Mountain acres. The railroad then was to be extended to the coal fields in Bernice in Sullivan County where it would connect with the State Line and Sullivan Railroad.

The corporation would control 94-square-miles in four counties—the largest tract of virgin forest remaining in Pennsylvania. It would yield two billion board feet of timber worth a net value of nearly two million English pounds. At this time an English pound was equivalent to $4.85 in American dollars. It would take 21 years to timber the 60,000 acres, with an average annual net yield to the corporation of 52,000 pounds, which was a 17 percent annual investment yield. In addition, a railroad hauling lumber, coal, and tannery hides would generate another 15,000 pounds annually. The corporation was to be financed by 400,000 shares at ten pounds each and seven percent mortgage debentures totaling 350,000 pounds.

For the next two years, the Ricketts lands were surveyed to determine their timber and mineral yields. With a single-minded determination to pursue the English plan, Ricketts deflected the interests of American lumbering firms also interested in portions of his tracts. There was a stream of letters and telegrams exchanged between Ricketts and his English and Philadelphia investors. In the midst of this fortune-gathering, Ricketts was offered the Democratic nomination for state governor in 1888, but he declined all interest in state politics and refused the offer. Instead, he did agree to serve as a member of the World's Columbian Fair Commission in Chicago, Illinois, to be held in 1893. Of course, too, he could not decline an important role as member of the Pennsylvania Gettysburg Monument Commission which was responsible for setting up war memorials at the battlefield.

Finally, on January 31, 1889, the Jamison syndicate and R. Bruce Ricketts agreed to sell their 60,000 joint acreage to the English corporation for $1,920,000. The sale was scheduled for completion on April 15, 1889. The sellers were to receive $950,000 in cash and $970,000 in shares in the English corporation. In every respect, the English plan met all of Ricketts' dreams, and in February 1889 the Central Pennsylvania Railway, Land and Timber Company, Ltd., was formed in London and it issued a proposed prospectus in May 1889 to raise the necessary financing. But the plan quickly fell apart. Marketing the plan fell on B.K. Jamison in Philadelphia who was unable to raise the nearly $2 million to complete the sale. There were factions within the company which disputed the method of financing the project. With the financial troubles that occurred, the bankers sought to interest Ricketts with less cash and more stock. But Ricketts was firm. He wanted at least $20 an acre in cash or its equivalent. Whether Ricketts' property should be purchased prior to completion of the Bloomsburg and Sullivan Railroad was another issue. A competing banking house from New York also entered the controversy, a natural consequence since a huge commission on a successful sale would follow. But English investors were not warm to a major underwriting with an American timber corporation without a proven business history, since other American lumbering com-

General Harry Clay Trexler (1854–1933) was born in Easton, Pennsylvania, the seventh generation of German pioneers who settled in the state in 1709. Raised in Allentown, Trexler was a partner with his father in the E. W. Trexler and Son lumber firm. In 1885 he married Mary M. Mosser, the only daughter of William K. Mosser, who was well-known in the tanning industry. H. C. Trexler was a remarkable entrepreneur, organizing the Lehigh Portland Cement Company, one of the largest cement producers in the world. He also was President of the Lehigh Valley Transit Company; he centralized the operations of the Pennsylvania Power and Light Company in Allentown, and he merged the Lehigh Valley's Consolidated Telephone Company with the Bell Telephone Company. He served since 1895 with the national guard under six Pennsylvania Governors, was Quartermaster General of the Pennsylvania National Guard in 1911, and retired from the service in April 1918 at age 65 with the rank of Brigadier General. His Lehigh Valley farming interests were immense and he created elk and bison game reserves to save the species. He also acquired 12,000 acres in Kidder Township, Carbon County, which he gifted to the state as Hickory Run State Park. The enviable Allentown park system is his creation. During his lifetime, he was the second wealthiest man in the state, and tenth in the nation. His father, E. W. Trexler, died in an accident at a railroad crossing near Emaus in July 1900. Henry C. Trexler died in November 1933 from injuries in an automobile accident. His will provided trusts for over seventy-five charitable institutions.

panies had already burned some English stockholders. Finally, the international money market softened in early 1890, a prelude to a major international recession, and financing the project was in serious jeopardy.

By the end of 1889, Ricketts realized the English deal may not succeed. The Bloomsburg and Sullivan Railroad had already reached Jamison City a year earlier in November 1888 where a major tannery and saw mill were in operation. But there were not any firm plans to extend the Jamison City railroad to Ricketts' lands. Moreover, the key principal in Jamison City, Col. James Corcoran, who operated the Fishing Creek Lumber Company there, had a fortune disappear in a June 1889 flood which destroyed his main lumber business in Williamsport. Even after the disaster, Corcoran was among the interested persons who sought to attract Ricketts into selling his land if the English plan were to fail. But Ricketts was wary of Corcoran, and shortly Corcoran was insolvent and he would be forced to sell his Jamison City lumber operation in 1891.

Ricketts extended the deadline to close the English deal through 1889 and into early 1890, but he was realizing only promises and not cash from the transaction. In the meantime, the State Line and Sullivan and the Wilkes-Barre and Harvey's Lake railroad lines were under construction and would cut through the North Mountain. He wisely sought an alternative cash flow from his timber tracts.

In January 1890, Ricketts began correspondence with E.W. Trexler and Son, an Allentown-based lumber firm which already had a substantial mill at Lopez, a few miles north of Lake Ganoga. Lopez was formerly known as Tar Bridge because the bridge crossing Lopez Creek was coated with a coal tar paint to preserve its lumber construction. One view claims it was renamed to commemorate John P. Lopez, a contractor of Spanish origin, who reputedly drowned working in the stream while working on the turnpike. Lopez boomed as a lumber town after 1885 when the State Line and Sullivan Railroad reached the Loyalsock Creek, drawing within a couple of years both the Jennings Brothers Lumber Company and the Trexler, Turrell, and Company.

E.W. Trexler and Son was an Allentown partnership composed of brothers Harry C. Trexler (1854–1933) and Edwin G. Trexler, and their father, E.W. Trexler (1826–1910), who retired from the firm in 1910. The firm had a national reputation in the lumber business. H.C. Trexler was a remarkable entrepreneur who organized major utility, transit, agriculture, cement, and lumbering operations. He eventually became one of the nation's richest men. In the Sullivan County operations in Lopez, J.H. Turrell of Tunkhannock joined the business as Trexler, Turrell, and Company. At Ricketts, the three men captioned the business Trexler and Turrell Lumber Company. Harry Trexler remained in Allentown while Edwin Trexler managed the early Lopez and Ricketts operations.

J. Henry Turrell (1850–1909) was raised near Sugar Run in Bradford County. He left the Wyalusing Academy at age seventeen to enter the lumber business in Sugar Run, later joining with Trexler to lumber in Lopez and Ricketts. He was known as "Cocky" Turrell; he also managed the operations at the Ricketts site. He was known for a long white beard which he kept inside his shirt. Sometimes he chewed on the end of his beard. After his death in

1909, J. Elmore Turrell took over his father's interest in the Trexler and Turrell Company in Ricketts.

Ricketts and Trexler representatives met at Long Pond in late January 1890. In the meantime, it was well rumored that the English deal was in trouble. Major lumber dealers in the mid-Atlantic area continued to express interest in Ricketts' lands, but Ricketts felt obligated to play out his agreement with the English syndicate. As a saving grace, however, Ricketts decided to lease portions of the timber land along Mehoopany Creek to the Trexler company. On April 4, 1890, Ricketts and Trexler signed an agreement which at least gave Ricketts an immediate $25,000 with the prospect of additional cash if the Trexler lease were continued in future years.

In late June 1890, Ricketts traveled to London with the hope of finally concluding the sale. He signed another agreement of sale, but only for 40,000 acres of his tracts. The latest survey indicated the Ricketts tracts contained 1.4 billion feet of lumber, about 400 million in various hardwoods such as birch, beech, ash, maple, and occasional cherry, and one billion feet in the softwoods, hemlock and spruce. This time Brown Brothers and Company, a New York City banking firm, was in the deal. But the B.K. Jamison bank in Philadelphia was still listed as the formal American banker. The new corporation was titled the Penn-

J. H. Turrell is shown in later life, but with a shorter beard than remembered by Ricketts' workmen.

sylvania Land and Lumber Company, Ltd., and financed by 60,000 shares at five pounds each and six percent mortgage debentures totaling 150,000 pounds. Ricketts would receive $960,000 of which $637,500 was cash and $242,500 in mortgage debentures in the company. Now, the annual return for each of 24 years was estimated at 52,000 pounds for a 15 percent annual investment yield. The local newspapers proclaimed Ricketts a millionaire. But the financial market was not improving and creditors were after Ricketts, along with borrowers who read of Ricketts' fortune. But the August 25 settlement date passed and still the sale was not completed.

In October 1890, Albert Lewis, the lumber king of Wyoming Valley, traveled to England to secure a lease of the Ricketts' lands from the English syndicate. While his principal operations were along the Lehigh River, his Lehigh Valley Railroad associates were ready to add the Ricketts' tract to their Bowman's Creek lands which they were timbering in Alderson at Harvey's Lake, and in Stull by the following year. Lewis, too, already had portable mills in Sullivan County on small tracts he had leased earlier. But Lewis must have realized in England that the entire English plan was questionable. He returned to the United States without a lease from the English.

By the end of the year, the proposed English corporation appeared hopeless. The B.K. Jamison banking house in Philadelphia,

Col. R. Bruce Ricketts is shown in later life, the most well-known portrait of the North Mountain land baron.

which until the last moment had still hoped to carry the deal, became insolvent in late November 1890 and by May 1891 Jamison was asking Ricketts for a $500 loan.

By mid-1891, Ricketts knew the English deal had fully collapsed; his close friends similarly advised him and Ricketts moved quickly to salvage his situation. In late June 1891, Ricketts and the Mehoopany Mining and Manufacturing Company agreed to sell its tracts in Wyoming and Sullivan counties, which now totaled 16,000 acres, to tanning company agents known as Davidge and Crary, at the $20-an-acre Ricketts always wanted. The tanning and leather syndicate purchasers were associated with the Jennings Brothers lumber firm in Lopez which would timber the lands until early 1905.

The Mehoopany Mining and Manufacturing Company, generally composed of Col. R. Bruce Ricketts, the E.P. Darling estate, the Michael Meylert estate, W.E. Little, a Tunkhannock lawyer, and Henry W. Palmer, a Luzerne County judge, sold their lands to Davidge and Crary on July 1, 1893, for $310,000. As expected, Davidge and Crary resold the lands to the Union Tanning Company in 1894. With the 1893 sale, Ricketts would have finally realized some profit from his investments. This sale and the 1876 Bowman's Creek sale to Albert Lewis and the Lehigh Valley Railroad were the only two major sales Ricketts realized in his lifetime.

As late as June 1891, the English group was still enticing Ricketts with a revised plan, but now for 20,000 acres of his land. But Ricketts could not receive any earnest money from the English investors to continue an option on the Ricketts tracts, only the promise of increased stock participation in any English plan.

During the 1890 season, the Trexler firm proved very reliable. They had located and built a mill on the Mehoopany Creek, the site of the town of Ricketts, and could cut at least ten million board feet annually on Ricketts' lands. The English plan had failed and in April 1891 Ricketts renewed his contract with Trexler and Turrell, a relationship which would continue until the close of lumbering at Ricketts in 1913.

With the pronouncements in the newspapers that Col. Ricketts was a millionaire from his land deals, which were untrue but never quite retracted, Ricketts began to enjoy an increased social prominence sometimes denied to him earlier when he was "land poor." The Ganoga Lake Branch of the Lehigh Valley Railroad brought a stream of social and business guests to the Ricketts estate from the early 1890s until his death in 1918. Col. Ricketts still owned his mansion on South River Street in Wilkes-Barre, now a Wilkes University dormitory, but in the summer months Ricketts continually entertained at the Stone House. The Stone House served as a hotel until the end of the 1903 season, after which Ricketts was the genial host for personal guests and business friends at the Ganoga estate in the summer months. During the balance of the year, R. Bruce and Elizabeth Ricketts lived in Wilkes-Barre. He held weekly gatherings of the community's judicial and economic elite at the home, and his only career was tending to the management of his properties. However, his friend, Judge Stanley Woodward, did prevail upon Col. Ricketts to accept an appointment as Wilkes-Barre City Treasurer in April 1898, a post he held until April 1902.

In declining health for two years, Col. Robert Bruce Ricketts died at 8:00 a.m. on November 13, 1918, at his Lake Ganoga home.

He was largely remembered in his obituary for the heroic stand of July 2, 1863. But his wide circle of friends remembered him for his gentle soul, wide-reading, quiet charity and his love of nature. Six days later his widow, Elizabeth Reynolds Ricketts, to whom the Colonel was married for fifty years, quietly passed away at the family home in Wilkes-Barre. She had been widely identified with several community organizations, where her special charm drew easy friendships and her family devotion was widely admired. They were buried in a simple, barely-cleared family cemetery in the woods near where the Ganoga log railroad station once stood.

The Town of Ricketts (1890-1913)

The town of Ricketts arose at a site on the Wyoming–Sullivan County border along Mehoopany Creek. It was chosen in the summer of 1890 by the Trexler and Turrell Lumber Company, which had contracted to cut about 5,000 acres of virgin forest land near Lake Ganoga that was owned by Col. R. Bruce Ricketts of Wilkes-Barre. At the same time, Ricketts also leased a smaller tract adjacent to Trexler's tracts for timbering to Albert Lewis, another major lumber manufacturer who was building or acquiring mills in the region in Mehoopany, Lopez, Stull, Harvey's Lake, and Dallas.

The center of the ghost town of Ricketts today is located 4.4 miles north of the present park entrance to Lake Jean at Ricketts Glen State Park on Route 487. Here, immediately below the Pennsylvania Fish Commission access road which bears right to Mountain Springs, a small bridge crosses Mehoopany Creek. To the right of the site, before crossing the bridge, there was once a street lined with homes, a church, and a lodge hall. The bridge site was roughly the location of a dam which impounded creek water in "downtown" Ricketts in Forkston Township in Wyoming County. The mill pond here supported, over time, at least four different mills. Immediately on the other side of the Route 487 bridge, a railroad bed to the right leads past an area along the creek once alive with the workings of mills. A little further up the rail bed there once bloomed a commercial center with a railroad station, company store, hotel, school, and company houses.

In the other direction, upstream from the bridge on Route 487, about three-quarters of a mile into Colley Township in Sullivan County, was another more substantial log dam and pond which once impounded countless logs for the huge Trexler and Turrell lumber mill. Here, at "uptown" Ricketts, surrounding the mill, were auxiliary buildings: for example, the blacksmith shop, planing mill, and grease house, which served the mill works. In the neighborhood there were other house-filled streets, barns, and a two-room Sullivan County schoolhouse, a substantial community which disappeared nearly eighty years ago.

This Ranald Douglas postcard view dated 1908 was taken from the belfry of the Ricketts Lutheran Church and overlooks downtown Ricketts. Along Church Row the Turrell house sits on the right; at the bottom of the hill the white house was leased to the company physician. Mehoopany Creek and the lower mill pond cannot be viewed, but the downtown mills crowd the interior of the photograph. The Ricketts hotel sits on a hill in the top center of the view. Douglas photographs are usually indicated by his printing and initials on the face of the card.

A bark pile sits to the left of the woods crew at Gil Lathrop's camp six miles east of Ricketts. Trees in the left background have a "butt ring" removed prior to cutting. The logs in the foreground have been peeled and are ready for cutting into lengths. The third man from the left has a peavey to turn logs. The last man on the right has a bark peeler's spud.

During the summer of 1890, Albert Lewis built a water-powered mill in lower Ricketts over Mehoopany Creek, in Wyoming County, but his operations here would only last until 1894. Lewis's partner in this early operation was F.L. Sittser. Their firm may have floated logs from Splashdam Pond, located on a nearby tributary, to their millsite on the creek near the county line. More importantly, in the same 1890 summer, the Trexler firm was building a more substantial steam-driven mill a short distance upstream from the Lewis site in Sullivan County. The timber leases with Col. Ricketts to lumber in the area were originally limited to the immediate tracts surrounding Lake Ganoga, since Ricketts had planned to sell most of his land, 45,000 acres, to a British syndicate. But by April 1891, the sale collapsed and the Trexler firm, with whom Ricketts had confidence, had its contract continued, a relationship which would last another 22 years.

The Trexler company devoted the 1890 season to mill construction, allied buildings, labor retention, and initial timbering activities. Too, railroad lines to Ricketts were still under construction and lumber stock would have to be either hauled to Lopez or stockpiled until the railroad to markets was opened. Trexler planned to harvest 5 million feet in 1890, and 12 million feet in 1891, with a "stumpage fee" totaling $50,000 to Col. Ricketts for 1890 and 1891.

Building the Town

The community of Ricketts was quickly built over the next three years, particularly after the main railroad line from Towanda to Wilkes-Barre was opened in 1893, along with the Ganoga Lake branch line from the mill town to the summer resort at the lake.

The town began to bloom as 1891 opened. In January 1891 a

A woods crew and teams surround a log slide, probably at Trexler and Turrell's South Mountain operation near Kasson Brook, above Stull. Log slides were not in general use at Ricketts. The mule teams haul the logs to the trough and the logs slide by gravity to a railroad loading site, or they slide directly to a mill pond.

Ricketts post office designation was established, initially in Sullivan County, but it was moved to the company store in Wyoming County in November 1891 with E.G. Trexler as postmaster. The town hosted the two saw mills of Lewis and Trexler, a company store, barber shop, and a growing population. J.R. Pennington, a Lopez butcher, opened a meat market at Ricketts in competition with the company store, but was ousted by the Trexler firm. By September, a schoolhouse—presumably the Sullivan County school—was under construction at uptown Ricketts, the lot a gift of Col. Ricketts. It would be followed by a second school in downtown Ricketts in Wyoming County. A three-mile road from Jamison City to Ganoga Lake was underway. It was constructed down the mountain as a public road and as a route to haul hemlock bark from the Ricketts tracts to a tannery in Jamison City.

During the early months of 1892, a Loyalsock Railroad crew of eighty men, commanded by J. Ross Rahm, was building the last couple of miles of railroad between Ricketts and its terminus at Bean Run, where it would connect with Albert Lewis's log railroad which was under construction from Noxen. The Loyalsock crew slept and boarded in railroad cars as they built the railroad one mile at a time. When a mile of track was completed, a construction train and supplies were moved up to a new construction site. The gang moved forward to cut down trees, another followed to clean the debris away, and a third crew followed to blow out stumps with dynamite. Meanwhile, D.B. Cope, railroad boss for Albert Lewis, was completing the line from Noxen, and the two lines could have been quickly joined by March 1892. However, Lewis, who actually constructed his log line for sale to the Lehigh Valley Railroad, would not permit connection of the two

railroad systems until business disputes with the Lehigh Valley were settled. Through 1892 and mid-1893, trains would only run south from Towanda to Ricketts.

A full season of activity dawned the spring of 1892 for the town of Ricketts. New men were arriving in town to work. There was a housing shortage and more company homes were planned. There was not a shortage of dogs or rats, however, and it was suggested that the place should be renamed "Dogtown." Trexler was moving rail ties into the woods for logging lines and crews were cutting tracks to bring out bark, and peeling would begin in late May. On May 8, 1892, the Ricketts Sunday School was formed at the schoolhouse. George Thrasher, from Albany, Pennsylvania, opened a shoemaker shop in Ricketts and the company hired W.B. Hoffa from Bernice as a butcher. Burton Douglas signed a one-year contract to carry the mail between Ricketts and Lopez for $300.

The woods were active with trail blazing, the running of log rail lines, and workmen at various jobs in the forests. In June 1892, there was a bark camp near Ricketts and also at the Barnes and Kipper sites. Lumber and bark camps were named after either the camp boss or a well-known site. The Sweeney lumber camp house burned in mid-June and the men lost everything except the work clothes they were wearing. The company tore out stalls in a barn and installed bunks for the men for shelter.

A defiant Ricketts woods crew display their drinking outside a crude lumber camp house. Drinking and smoking in the woods were prohibited, but, of course, regularly occurred. Ricketts, however, was a relatively peaceful community and the woodsmen were not remembered as troublesome.

By January 1893, the Trexler company had graded the nearly four-mile branch line from the saw mill at Ricketts to a log-house station at Lake Ganoga, but the opening of the Lehigh Valley Railroad line through Ricketts was delayed after nearly five feet of snow fell in late February. The snow was still three-feet deep in mid-April. In early May the Hotel Ricketts, 40-feet wide and 60-feet long, was opened with F.D. Shantz from Newfoundland, Pennsylvania, as the manager. Heavily-built and talkative, Shantz would be quite successful as "landlord" of the popular hotel built on the crest of a small rise overlooking the company store and downtown mills. The lumber men were anxious to have a hotel in town to buy beer; dances were held Saturday nights in a community hall, and it was a nuisance hauling beer from Lopez which was a "wild" town and permitted alcohol sales. Undoubtedly, the men grumbled incessantly when Col. Ricketts insisted his town and the hotel would remain "dry," with the tacit approval of the Trexler firm. Another tale holds, however, that the Ricketts House originally did sell beer. But workmen were only paid at the end of the month. If a workman was employed in mid-month, he was paid in groceries from the company store until regular monthly paychecks began. But some men would swap groceries from the store for beer or liquor at the hotel. One day someone substituted sand for sugar that was illicitly traded for beer. The sand ended up in "Cocky" Turrell's oatmeal for breakfast at the hotel, and the "boss man" thereafter ordered a "dry" town.

By mid-1893, there was talk of the railroad from Towanda to

Wilkes-Barre finally opening. In the meantime, the town was alive with humming saws, crashing boards, and rumbling rail cars. Along the hillsides, small armies of men crept over piles of lumber everywhere—and in mid-May it would sometimes still snow. The Lehigh Valley Railroad finally settled with Lewis, and the through line from Wilkes-Barre and Harvey's Lake to Towanda was opened on July 1, 1893. The mill town of Ricketts could finally boom with all outlets open by rail traffic. At his Lake Ganoga estate, Ricketts' brother, Frank, deaf from a childhood bout with scarlet fever, managed the North Mountain House, catering to an increasing summer resort business. In fact, as the trolley and train lines were opening Harvey's Lake as a resort for the general public, Ricketts' Ganoga estate was becoming the fashionable, private resort for the Wyoming Valley money crowd. General lumbering within a half-mile of Lake Ganoga was prohibited, but while clearing for building lots near the hotel in October 1893, workmen cut down a hemlock tree six feet in diameter. A ring count indicated the tree was 532 years old.

Ricketts was not a seasonal community. The mills generally ran all year. In the winter months, snow was actually welcome. Logs would be easily skidded on the snow to be piled along the railroad. Otherwise, it was extra work to haul the logs in a dry winter season. Skating parties were the most popular form of recreation at Lake Ganoga or sometimes at the mill dams or local ponds. In November, the hunting season opened, but lumbering and hunting would annihilate the deer by 1912, when the last native deer was reportedly killed. For the indoor crowd, a literary society, mostly for the women, was formed in January 1894. The Sunday School seemingly had failed and the following month a new one was organized with E.G. Trexler as superintendent; with the company boss as head, the townspeople would have to attend—even if the temperature did hit 30 degrees below zero the last Sunday in February 1894.

Ricketts, unlike Stull, used a Barnhart loader, a steam-operated device, to pick up logs and load them onto Trexler and Turrell's log railroad for shipment to the Ricketts mill. Bark from hemlock trees was removed from the trees prior to the shipment and milling process.

Church services were held every second Sunday at 10:30 a.m. at the schoolhouse with an Evangelical preacher from Dushore. In March 1894, the communities of Bernice, Lopez, Ricketts, and Shinerville were organized into a separate Bernice and Lopez Circuit, and a novice, but well-liked minister, Rev. F.H. Foss, formerly a printer, provided services to Ricketts on Thursday evenings.

Several well-known community members were already in place by May 1894. William Colt managed the company store, assisted by Lorin Tresslar. Colt would move to Pittston in 1895 to be replaced by Tom Kennedy. G.M. Peet was a company blacksmith; Joshua Zacharias had the meat market and managed a boarding house. The principal saw filer at the big mill was J.C. Dyer. James Hadsell had charge of sixty men at the lath mill. Lath were narrow strips of wood used to support plastered walls in home construction. In one day the lath mill alone was cutting 87,000 feet of lumber, producing 30,000 pieces of lath daily; if laid end-to-end, it would stretch nearly 23 miles.

During the winter of 1894–1895, Albert Lewis left the Ricketts area. The Albert Lewis mill in Ricketts, which may have been largely idle for two years, was dismantled in December 1894, and the machinery relocated to Lewis's mill operations in Crellin, West Virginia. Lewis, of course, was extremely active at Stull and Harvey's Lake with his own lumbering and ice-cutting operations along Bowman's Creek, and did not pursue any future business arrangement with Col. Ricketts. There was an undisclosed, strained relationship or rivalry between them, perhaps due to Lewis's advantage in the ice business at Bear Creek. Ricketts may have decided to retain the advantage in the incredible lumber business Ricketts and Trexler shared at North Mountain.

There were two additional enterprises added to North Mountain. Trexler and Col. Ricketts formed an ice company which

In another Douglas view, the right hand head saw of the log carriage has cut two sides of a log in the "squaring" process. In the background is the circular saw and the sawyer and observers. Later the mill converted to "band saws." The two men on the carriage controlled "dogs," which were semi-circular clamps to hold the log in place during the sawing process.

erected an 80 by 100-foot ice house near the railroad station at Lake Ganoga, and by January 1895 the company's 175 men were cutting and shipping a large number of railroad cars of ice to Philadelphia and New York markets. The Lehigh Valley Railroad was also a major buyer of ice to be used in hauling meat and perishables. The business was so successful that the Ganoga Lake Ice Company was incorporated on April 21, 1897, by J.H. Turrell, H.C. Trexler, William R. Ricketts, G.H. Heintzelman, and E.G. Trexler. The ice company was partly formed to provide Col. Ricketts' son, William, an enterprise of his own to manage. The Colonel's trusted servant, John H. Green, was also active in the daily management of the company.

Trexler and Turrell also expanded its operations in December 1895 to a mill they erected in Noxen after purchasing 1,100 acres of Sullivan and Wyoming County timberlands, which Col R. Bruce Ricketts owned with other business associates. This sale followed an earlier report in January 1895 that Trexler and Turrell had planned to purchase 15,000 acres of lands from Col. Ricketts. But these accounts are in error. In 1895, Col. Ricketts only intended to lease an additional 15,000 acres to Trexler for timbering in the Mehoopany Lands, selling 1,100 acres to Trexler in a more removed area serviced by Trexler's Noxen mill. For a time Trexler and Turrell also had a small mill at Kasson Brook, north of the immediate Ricketts tracts. In late 1896, the Trexler firm sold its Lopez operations to Jennings Brothers.

Other business and community pieces were also joining the town fabric. A popular lodge in rural areas in the 1890s was the Patriotic Order of the Sons of America. A POS of A Hall was built at Ricketts around 1896, the first building north of the Lutheran Church. The initiation rites were usually harmless tricks. A shoeless, blindfolded candidate would be led down a corridor while the men hit his toes and head with "sawdust clubs"—tubes of muslin filled with sawdust. The blindfold was removed and the candidate could see another member heating a branding iron. The blindfold was replaced again and a long wait followed. As the candidate was expecting the branding iron, a piece of ice was sent down the back of his neck. Then the candidate would have to stand on a short step ladder where he was told the floor was strewn with broken glass and nails. When ordered to jump, he was caught in a blanket and tossed around. The rites concluded after the new member kissed a picture of a jackass. Thereafter, he was a full-fledged member of the humorously-named "Arabian Degree Klan" of the Ricketts POS of A order. The order had 30 to 40 members; it was a social club but members could also buy sickness, accident, and life insurance through the club.

After construction of the POS of A Hall, community dances, formerly held at the town hall, were moved to the lodge house. Dance music was simple, usually a fiddle and organ. Traveling medicine and lantern slide shows were shown at the hall, and Baptist and Methodist Church services were also held there.

On March 8, 1897, the St. John Evangelical Lutheran Church was organized at Ricketts. The Rev. Christian Krahmer of Noxen was named pastor. The building, 32-feet wide and 48-feet long, was erected during the year and was consecrated on Sunday, December 4, 1897, when the final $60 to pay for it was collected. Rev. J.L. Miller succeeded Krahmer at this time.

Extra band saws were stored along the ceiling of the sawyer's room at the Ricketts mill.

On October 12, 1897, the Ricketts Manufacturing Company was formed to operate an excelsior mill in downtown Ricketts at the site of the Lewis mill. G.N. Ruff from Allentown relocated to Ricketts to operate the new mill. Excelsior was a form of packaging material made from shredded spruce wood. The excelsior mill only ran about three years. The site was later reconstructed for a stave and barrel head mill until the town closed.

The main sawmill in uptown Ricketts originally had a circular saw—about six feet in diameter. Then, a band saw joined the circular saw. In 1898, the Ricketts sawmill eliminated the circular saw and added a second band saw increasing its capacity to 100,000 feet daily. One, or usually two, log trains made regular trips each day to the mill pond. On its logging railroad in the woods and at the mills, Trexler and Turrell used two Climax locomotives weighing 25 tons each. The first Climax was purchased in 1893 after Trexler's initial second-hand locomotive was wrecked in the May 1893 accident. A second Climax was purchased in 1895. In 1901, the company purchased a 37-ton Heisler, followed by a 70-ton Shay locomotive in 1902, with the company purchasing their last locomotive, another Climax, at an uncertain later date. By 1900, the complete community was in place and extremely productive until the abrupt close of operations when the timber reserves were depleted 13 years later.

The community itself referred to the lower mill complex in Wyoming County as "downtown" and the main sawmill area in Sullivan County as "uptown." The initial mill downtown was the Albert Lewis mill. After Lewis left Ricketts in 1895, the sequence of mill operations in downtown is not precisely known. An excelsior mill was located here for a few years (1897–c.1900), but the principal

mill was the Trexler stave and barrel head mill. The Lewis mill was converted to these operations by the Trexler and Turrell company. Certainly, for a time, the old Lewis mill was used to air-dry staves. After the stave mill fire in 1908, air-drying sheds were constructed across the creek. In 1909, a grist mill was also built in downtown to provide feed for the Trexler horse and mule teams used in the timbering industry.

Further up the track in downtown Ricketts were the company store, the Ricketts train station, a section foreman house, a barber shop, and a footbridge over the creek to the old town hall, which was converted at a later date to a company house. On the hill, of course, was the hotel. At this site, the Bowman's Creek Branch entered the town and split into a "Y." The main line turned right to Lopez; the 3.85-mile Ganoga Lake spur line ran along the creek from the downtown area, 1.45 miles to the main sawmill at uptown, and 2.4 miles to the Ganoga Lake station. The Trexler logging lines generally ran off the Ganoga Branch railroad line, but Trexler also had trackage rights over a section of the main railroad line from Ricketts east to Opperman Pass, a distance of two miles. Trexler would have run additional log rail lines from this stretch of Lehigh Valley track.

In the area behind the company store, on a hill overlooking the downtown mills, was additional company housing. For a time, there was also a one-room Wyoming County school, smaller than the Sullivan County school, only a short distance away.

The center of downtown Ricketts had the company store and post office on the left, the Ricketts station in the center, and the Ricketts hotel on the hill.

On the other side of the creek in Wyoming County, along a street named Church Row, there was a line of homes including the company physician's house, the substantial Turrell home, and the Lutheran Church. Here, too, began a series of homes occupied by skilled employees, the mill wrights, sawyers, and saw filers. This area has been partially dozed out and landmarks no longer can be traced. But Whipple Street, named after George "Zeke" Whipple, the "woods boss"—a middle manager—may have begun here, crossing into Sullivan County, with Mill Street shooting off towards the big dam and the sawmill.

In the Whipple Street area was located the POS of A Hall, the Sullivan County school, and additional homes along Mill Street for the "higher ups." There was also a large barn on Mill Street which handled fifty teams of horses. Finally, the big sawmill was located at the head of the crib-dam on Mehoopany Creek, a small industrial area crowded with rail lines, lumber yards to the rear, and service buildings—including the blacksmith's shop, and in later years separate planing and lath mills—beyond which there was additional housing for mill workers.

Life in the Woods

A crew blazed out main roads into the forest, followed by cross roads between them. Two man crews—a fitter and a spudder—would work between the main roads. In the hemlock forests this

The stave mill and pond is shown in another Douglas photo. The area is crowded with timber, generally spruce, to cut into staves for barrel making.

work occurred in the early spring because sap running in the trees made stripping bark easier. The bark on the hemlock trees was stripped to sell to area tanning firms. Bark from other trees was not marketable and was not stripped. The crew initially cut a "butt ring" from the hemlock tree, a three-foot strip of the bark around the lower tree, which made sawing the tree easier. Using a cross-cut saw, the men cut through the butt ring and felled the tree. They would cut the top off from the fallen tree and then slit rings around the bark every four feet to the butt or sawed end. The tree tops were not harvested but left to rot. The fitter would then move to another standing tree to cut a "butt ring," while the spudder, using a special tool, peeled off the bark on both sides of the fallen tree in roughly three or four-foot high sheets. The bark could fall away in a single sheet from around the tree but most often it tore off in two or three pieces. Limbs, too, would have to be chopped off with an ax.

The bark was left for a time to flatten and dry out. Later it was gathered and pitched into piles of one cord each along the road. The crew was expected to cut four cords of bark daily. The bark was either taken by train in special cars designed for bark-hauling or loaded into wagons and hauled to area tanneries, for example, Noxen, Jamison City, Powell, and Elkland. The barking process ended in late July and early August and did not resume again until the following spring.

The felled trees generally lay in the woods to dry out until the late fall or winter when they were taken by various methods to the mill. In the meantime, crews had to "flog knots"—trim the trees of knots to make them relatively smooth so the horse teams could haul them. After flogging, the log cutters, a three-man crew, entered the woods. One man measured the trees and marked them for cutting into various lengths. He could also help cut away underbrush around the fallen timber. The two sawyers followed to cut the trees with cross-cut saws.

Trexler and Turrell had about fifty horse teams which were used in the woods. Wagon hauling in the woods could be arduous work. Sometimes "corduroy" roads paved with half-logs were built to keep wagon loads of bark or logs from getting stuck in wet areas. Heavy

On the opposite side of the track, across the creek from the Ricketts hotel, was the old town hall. A bridge over the creek led to it.

wagons could also overrun and crush a horse-team trying to haul a wagon load down a steep mountainside—particularly true for the steep descent of bark shipments into Jamison City. Rope and pulley rigs were sometimes used to hold wagons and guide their descent down the mountains. More often special devices using chains to lock up wagon wheels were used to brake the wagon's descent.

Throughout the forests there were crude trails built which patterned the mountainsides. Horse teams traveling the "skid trails" hauled the logs on wagons to a log slide, stream, or railroad site for shipment to the mill. If enough timber could not support construction of a railroad spur line, horse teams sledded out the timber on the winter snow when it was more efficient. A log slide was a wooden chute in which logs were placed and slid to a piling site. From 1890 to 1892 before the railroad was built, a log slide was used to shoot logs to the Ricketts mill pond. Thereafter, log slides were generally not used at Ricketts with the exception apparently in one or two outlying areas. A swollen spring stream or "splash dam" could float logs to a mill pond, and was used by the Albert Lewis firm in Ricketts and Stull in its early logging operations. Once the Ganoga branch of the Lehigh Valley Railroad was operational at Ricketts, log railroad spurs were built from it by the Trexler and Turrell Lumber Company. These spur lines went into the forests all over the North Mountain area.

At various rail sites, the timber was loaded in Trexler and Turrell's log trains. Trexler had five locomotives over a period of time after its first locomotive was damaged in 1893. Logs could be manually dumped into the railroad cars from temporary inclines built along the track, but on heavy jobs or major sites a "Barnhart" loader was used. This steam-driven machinery was fitted on rails on top of the log railroad cars. It picked up the logs and loaded them on cars, filling the train from the rear cars up to the front cars of the train.

Life in the Camps

The camp house was constructed from rough, unfinished boards from the company mill. Tar paper covered the exterior; rolls of brown or red building paper covered the inside walls. On the first floor there was a kitchen and large dining room with tables running the length of it, with hardwood benches for seats. After a ten or twelve-hour shift, which began at 7:00 a.m., the men poured into the camp house. The food was usually plain with plenty of potatoes, canned vegetables, and salt-cured meats. Wild fowl was a treat if available in the summer. Some camps raised pigs which ran loose until butchered in the late fall when pork would be served. A plain second room with a pot-bellied stove and hardwood benches along the walls served as a gathering place or recreation room. A sand box near the stove and buckets of sand around the room served as spittoons for the men who chewed tobacco.

The second floor served as the bunk house with beds two and three decks high made of rough lumber. The camp operator or family could also have separate quarters upstairs. Some beds had mattresses, but most beds were lined with hemlock or spruce boughs. Bed bugs and lice were a common problem, and in the spring the men would stock the beds outside, burn them, and build new beds.

Unlike the town of Ricketts, the woods camps attracted many immigrant laborers, particularly "Hungarians," a convenient phrase which encompassed several East European nationalities. German and Italian immigrants were more easily identified. There is some evidence that the camps could sometimes be segregated by nationality, forming a community with shared language, food preparations, and ethnic manners, and presided over by a work foreman who had some skill in the crew's native language. The available evidence, however, does not suggest either ethnic hostility or rivalry among the immigrant work camps.

The "wood hicks" paid for their room and board. A typical wage in 1906 was $1.60 a day working in the woods. Room and board cost 60¢ a day. Board included breakfast, noon dinner pail, and supper. If there were purchases at the company store for clothes, tobacco, or other items, these charges, too, were deducted from the employee's pay at the end of the month.

The old Lewis mill at downtown Ricketts was converted by Trexler and Turrell to a factory to make staves for barrels. Staves are packed upstairs and also outside to air-dry.

A typical boarding house served fifty men. The boarding house operator was an individual and helper or a married couple who contracted to run the house for whatever profit could be made. The house managers hired any additional help. The boarding operator purchased food from suppliers in Lopez or the Ricketts company store, which delivered it by a railroad hand car or the log train. Traveling butchers sold beef and lamb—13¢ a pound for beef. Food was cooked on one or two big stoves which had three lids across the top. The cook baked 30 to 35 loaves of bread a day and 10 to 15 pies. Breakfast was cereal, meat, potatoes, and pancakes. Fifty lunch pails were packed each morning for the men. Each contained four slices of bread, meat, cookies, fruit, and pie or cake. There was a filled coffee cup on top of the pail, but in the winter the coffee froze and the men were lucky if they could warm it enough to drink. After returning from the woods at the end of a winter day, the coffee was usually frozen solid and it would take a couple of hours to thaw out the lunch buckets to ready them for the next morning. Meat, potatoes, vegetables, and cake or pie was served for dinner—with lots of vegetable soup. A cellar, preferably near an underground spring, kept meat and vegetables relatively fresh.

On the left, Burt Schoonover is cutting dried stave blanks into beveled (curved) staves, while his helper on the right is packing them into bundles.

Fatal accidents and serious injuries were common in the lumber camps and mills. The earliest fatality at Ricketts was probably Frank Farrell, age 24, who was killed in May 1891 when a large limb of a maple tree he was cutting fell on him. In December 1891, Lincoln Ross died of injuries after a fall from a railroad car. In March 1892, the 18-month-old child of John Griegor was scalded in an accident at home and died. In June 1892, a limb fell on the shoulder of William H. Green, gashing him terribly, and he later died. A similar accident killed Michael Shay in January 1893. Saws and axes caused frequent injuries. Men fell from railroad

cars or were caught in mill machinery. A young man tried to change a gang saw in the main mill while some gears were still running—a process he saw the regular workmen do repeatedly without difficulty. But his pants got caught in the machinery and he bled to death. The loss of an arm or leg was not uncommon in timbering operations. Injured men were usually taken by train to the hospital at Sayre, in Bradford County, or sometimes to the General Hospital in Wilkes-Barre. The Ricketts community and the Trexler company made an annual contribution to the Sayre hospital for its medical services.

Ricketts did not have a cemetery. Lumber towns were not designed as long-term communities. The community people were often natives of nearby towns and deceased persons were sent to their hometowns for burial. John Sidelahn, an immigrant worker, was killed in July 1896 when he fell in front of a log train and two railroad cars ran over him. The immigrants from Eastern Europe were apparently superstitious, refusing to touch a deceased worker, and would not assume responsibility for the body. Invariably, burial arrangements for Hungarians were left to the charity of the settled townspeople—which oddly enough were sometimes called the "white folks" by the immigrants.

Particularly tragic deaths occurred in early 1914 at a Trexler and Turrell mill near Noxen the winter after their mill at Ricketts closed in 1913. On Saturday, February 14, 1914, Joseph Kelley and Jeremiah Sheehan, workers at the South Mountain camp of Trexler

At the top of Church Row was the Lutheran Church built in 1897.

and Turrell, walked five miles over snow-covered ground to Noxen for supplies. Unfortunately, they lingered in town until mid-afternoon. During the return tramp to camp, a blizzard overtook them and the temperature fell below zero, actually much colder due to a driving wind. The men were caught in the drifting snow and became exhausted. They eventually collapsed 300 feet apart and froze to death overnight only a short distance from their lumber camp. Their bodies were discovered by a search party the following morning. Kelley, age 50, handsome and deaf, was an unusual man. He was well-educated, a world traveler, and had been in the Navy. He may have been a professional boxer, which may have caused his deafness. He was also well-read, traveling to Noxen each Saturday to buy or borrow books and magazines and to enjoy a little time at a bar. When found frozen near a fallen tree trunk—a desperate refuge—he had clutched in his arms his favorite companions—books and magazines. The Kelley family buried him at Forkston, but Sheehan was a stranger to the community and he was buried by the local poor directors of Noxen.

Illnesses, too, especially during the severe winter months, took a toll. Particularly heart breaking were the deaths of infants and children. Arthur Harford, age 3, died of pneumonia in December 1895, as did Anna Hanke, age 9, who died of diptheria. A company blacksmith, G.M. Peet, lost his wife in May 1898 in childbirth. Peet shortly ran the following newspaper ad: "Wanted: A woman to take care of a four week old child. G.M. Peet, Box 85, Ricketts, Penna." Typhoid fever, from infected water, regularly occurred and was often fatal. In 1900, a typhoid epidemic occurred, along with a rash of pneumonia patients. The company physician this year was Dr. Frank Watkins. He and Walker Allen, the local barber, treated the patients, losing only two of their fifty patients.

The Sawmill Operations

The main Trexler and Turrell sawmill at uptown Ricketts on the Ganoga Branch was a major lumbering center in the region, second only to the Jennings mill in Lopez. In January 1895, Trexler employed 350 men who each earned $1.40 a day. The company had already cut 2 million feet of hemlock in the 1894–1895 season, with 4 million more feet to cut in the next few months. Trexler was nearly finished with earlier Lopez operations and would soon transfer its main office in Lopez and additional men to Ricketts.

The Trexler and Turrell mill at Ricketts had an easy capacity of 75,000 to 80,000 board feet daily and generally cut 10 to 12 million feet annually. In 1894, it was estimated the mill would manufacture 100 million feet of lumber during the life of the community, but eventually it would cut five times this amount. The Trexler and Turrell mill at Lopez could cut 50,000 feet daily. In Lopez, the Jennings Brothers mill was even larger, averaging 80,000 feet daily, 15 million feet annually, with immediate timber available for 125 million feet and additional tracts in sight. Another lumberer, Kipp, had a smaller mill at Newell, midway between Ricketts and Lopez. Kipp was cutting 50,000 feet daily with a reserve of 80 million feet. Sullivan County had an estimated 1.25 billion feet of hemlock timber alone, which lumberers were cutting at the rate of 110 million feet annually.

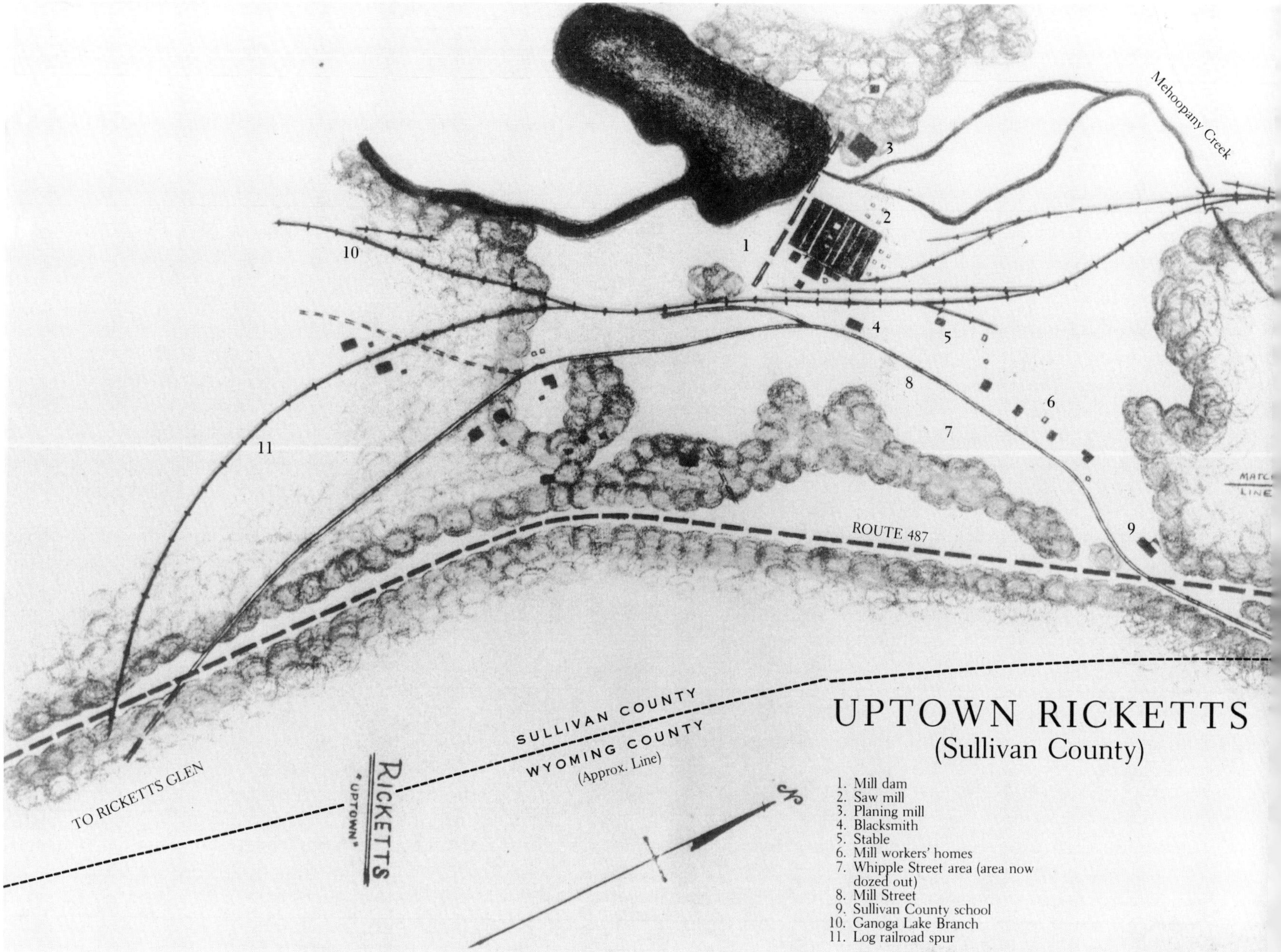
Mehoopany Creek
MATCH LINE
ROUTE 487
TO RICKETTS GLEN
SULLIVAN COUNTY
WYOMING COUNTY
(Approx. Line)
RICKETTS
"UPTOWN"
1
2
3
4
5
6
7
8
9
10
11
UPTOWN RICKETTS
(Sullivan County)
1. Mill dam
2. Saw mill
3. Planing mill
4. Blacksmith
5. Stable
6. Mill workers' homes
7. Whipple Street area (area now dozed out)
8. Mill Street
9. Sullivan County school
10. Ganoga Lake Branch
11. Log railroad spur

DOWNTOWN RICKETTS
(Wyoming County)

1. "Y" LVRR bears right to Lopez. Ganoga Lake Branch bears left.
2. LVRR station
3. T and T company store
4. Ricketts Hotel
5. Footbridge
6. Community Hall
7. Wyoming County school
8. Heintzelman house
9. Stave mill steam tunnels
10. Downtown mills
11. Stave mill dam and pond
12. Drying sheds
13. Turrell house
14. Lutheran Church
15. Church Row
16. Old road
17. P.O.S. of A. hall

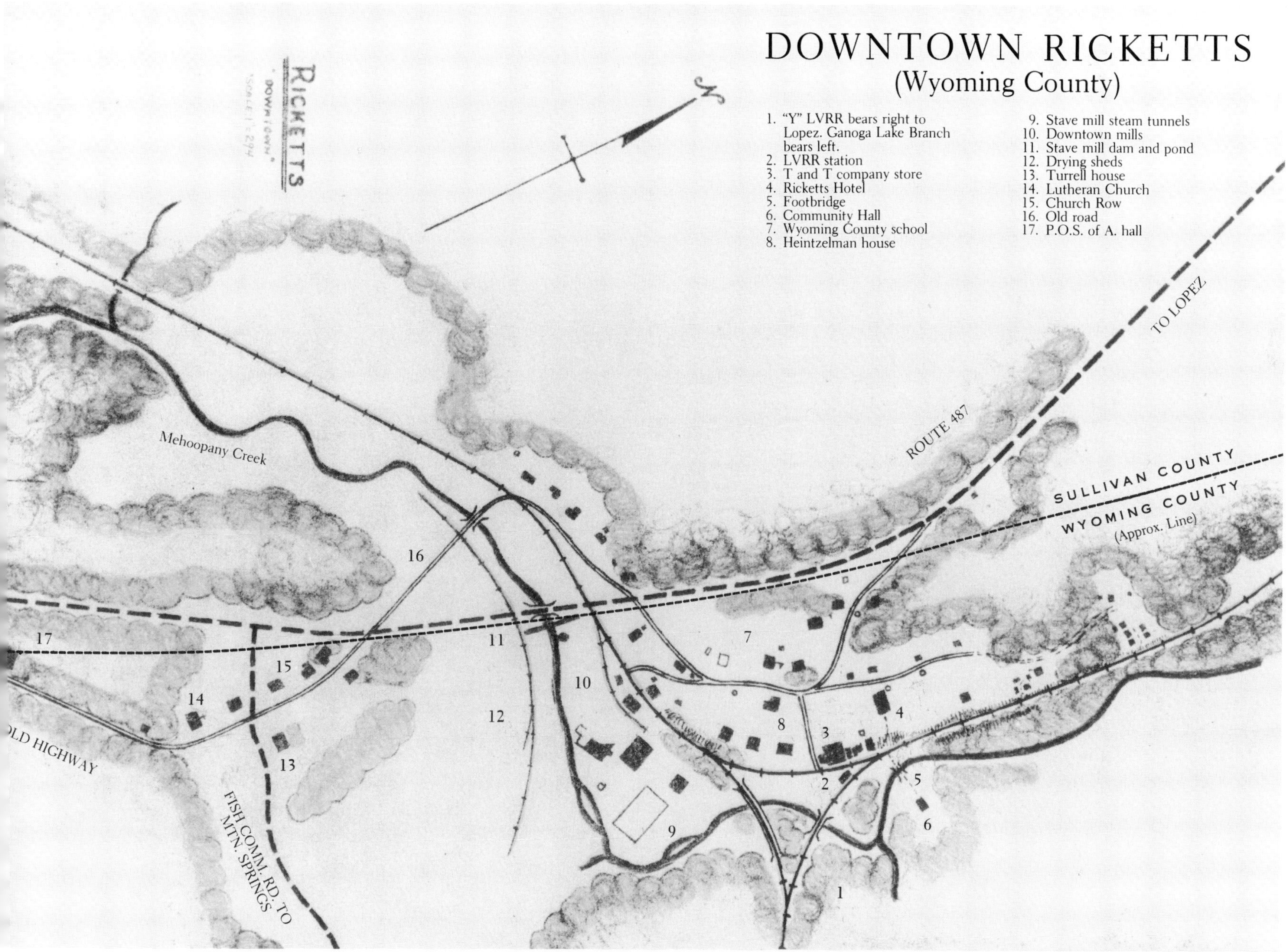

The home of Edgar Brown represented typical housing at Ricketts. Entire families lived in company homes. From left to right are Mabel Brown, age 4; Miss Cottman, a niece of Mrs. Brown; Mrs. Rockingham, another niece; Mrs. Catherine Brown; Ted Brown, age 14; Charles Brown, age 9; Lizzie Brown, age 12; William Brown, age 5; and Edgar Brown.

A detailed description of the Ricketts mill was not recorded. But it would have been similar to mills in the region at the time. After the harvested logs had been hauled and dumped into the Ricketts mill pond, they were sorted and moved by the pondman to the bottom of the jackslip (sometimes called "jackladder"), a ladder-like device which was inclined from the pond to the mill. The lugs on the endless chain of the jackslip would catch the logs and singly move them up the slip into the mill building. Logs were sent into the mill with the top or small end first. In some lumbering operations, the butt or large end contained the indented mark of the woods cutter, which was easily visible to a worker called the "scaler," while the log was still on the center deck above the mill opening. The scaler could then credit the log to the appropriate woods boss, who often worked in some lumbering operations on a commission basis for the lumber company. But at Ricketts, the commission system was apparently not in use and Trexler and Turrell is believed to have paid a standard wage to the various wood bosses.

The scaler immediately inside the mill controlled which way the log would be thrown from the center deck. Usually, the long logs were thrown to the right and the short logs to the left by a steam operated piston which came up through the center deck. The logs rolled right or left down the inclined log decks until they were stopped by a log loader, an 'L'-shaped device which rolled one log at a time onto the log carriage.

Two or three men stood on a log carriage which was a moveable 'shot-gun' or piston fed device similar to a large sled. The setter rode the front and the dogger rode the rear. The setter controlled one set of dogs (clamps) to fasten into the log. The dogger had

The Patriotic Order of Sons of America Hall is shown at uptown Ricketts in 1908.

two, and sometimes three, sets of dogs to fasten into the rear portions of the log.

The sawyer was responsible for the operation of the head saw, which initially cuts the timber trunks in order to maximize the lumber that can be cut from it. The sawyer stood near the head saw and controlled the log loader which flipped an individual log onto the carriage from the log deck. He also controlled a device which turned the log while it was on the carriage. The carriage with the two men moved forward, the head or band saw (or earlier a circular saw) stripped off one side of the log to begin the "squaring" process, and the carriage then retreated to its original position. By a signal to the men on the carriage, the sawyer told the men when to release the dogs so the log could be turned one-quarter way for a second side cut. In four or more passes, the log was "squared." The squared log was called a "cant." Near the sawyer's position, there was an order board which indicated what size lumber was needed to fill the company orders. The cant left the carriage and was then passed through a "gang saw," a series of circular saws on a drive shaft, which in one pass through the saws, cut the cant into a series of rough boards.

The tail-sawyer stood behind the gangsaw and picked off the newly sawed boards with a long metal "cant" hook, passing the boards onto the "live rolls" which was a powered conveyor belt system consisting of multiple rollers. This conveyed the cut lumber from the gangsaw to the edger, another smaller circular sawing operation which cut off the uneven edges and any remaining bark on the boards to produce lumber pieces with parallel edges. The edger man consulted another order board to see what width boards the company needed to fill orders. After setting the edger machine for the proper width, the board was fed into the machine. Wide boards were cut into two or more narrow boards for which there were orders.

Ordinarily, the sawmill process included a trimming process, a series of saws which cut the boards into uniform lengths. The boards were then marked into different grades of lumber and sorted for piling.

There were two other processes at the Ricketts mill. Certain lumber would have passed through the planing mill, which was added in 1898 and built behind the main sawmill. Here, certain rough dried lumber was finished by passing through a planer, a series of blades which give the boards a smooth surface before shipment.

Second, Ricketts also had a lath mill built behind the main mill. Edgings from the big mill, which were at least two inches thick, were run through gang saws that were four inches apart. Any scraps from this cutting were sent through the "hog" to fuel the boiler room fires or were sold at Lopez to make kindling wood. The edging slabs were then run through the "bolter" which cut each of them down to a uniform 1¼ by 1¼-inch size. These strips were then bundled and tied with twine. The bundles were then put through the "equalizer" saws and the lath cut to three or four foot lengths. Lath was a major commercial product used to support plastered walls in the home construction industry.

Lumber cut inside the mill was piled on small rail trucks. Boards of the same length were sorted and piled on the same truck. Several trucks were loaded at the same time. When they were full the trucks were pushed along the rails out of the mill to the pilers who either loaded the lumber into freight cars for shipment or piled it in the yards.

The pilers who stacked the lumber in the yard behind the mill wore heavy leather aprons and rude leather gloves. Each glove was made from a piece of heavy leather as wide as the palm of the hand with a strap around the wrist. It had no fingers in it nor was it made like a mitten. With use, the glove became slick as glass.

Lumber was stacked in a slightly tilted manner so rain would run off the boards much like a sloping roof. Boards were not completely stacked one on top of the other. Boards were placed between courses of lumber so air could circulate through the pile and dry the lumber. In the summer, it was cool between the piles, giving the men some relief from the heat.

Inside the mill, other operations were also necessary. Wood scrap, which was considerable, would be piled in railroad cars and

The Sullivan County school was originally one-room but became a double-room schoolhouse. The older section appears to be on the left.

taken to Lopez to make kindling wood. Ricketts did not have a kindling wood factory. In Lopez, small blocks of relatively uniform-sized wood were cut, bundled together, and tied with a tarred, flammable string with a paper tag attached to it. Kindling wood was sold by the millions in the cities to light coal stoves. The tag was lit; it fired the tarred string; the string fired the wood; the wood fired the coal in the stove.

At Ricketts the scrap pieces, unusable slabs and edging from the lumber and lath boards not sold for kindling, were dropped through the main floor of the mill to a conveyor which took them to the slasher that sawed them into short pieces. They were then conveyed to the hog which ground them into sawdust and chips. This refuse was conveyed to the sawdust storage area in the boiler room where it was burned. Sawdust from the mill operations was cleaned up about four times a day. Firemen worked the boilers day and night, usually in two shifts.

The saw filer was second only to the sawyers in pay. The saw filer's room was located to one side of the Ricketts mill in a separate room. He was responsible for sharpening the saws. One experienced filer could keep a double band-saw mill in operation. Racks along the ceiling of one end of the room stored extra saws. Saws were changed two to four times a day.

The Downtown Mills

In addition to the main sawmill uptown, there were also other substantial downtown milling operations. During the life of Ricketts, there was an incredible market for barrels, which were the most common form of packaging for all forms of farm produce and manufactured products. Barrels were made from curved strips of wood called staves, and round wooden tops and bottoms, fitted together and held in place with wire. Indeed, barrel production in the United States did not even peak until 1900.

There were three grades of staves. Number 1 staves were very tightly fitted for sugar and flour barrels; number 2 staves were used for cement and other products; and number 3 staves were used for potatoes and more loose products.

Mill Street ran into uptown Ricketts. H. A. Barnhart was standing on the porch at the far right when he was fatally struck by a flying brick from the boiler explosion in April 1909.

Ricketts had a major stave and barrel head factory built in 1898 at the downtown log pond. Spruce or other softwood was used for barrel-making. Short logs were cut into 30-inch lengths and quartered into "bolts" by a circular "bolting" saw. The mill could produce 60,000 bolts daily. The bolts were loaded on small cars and railed into a separate two-tiered building—the steam tunnels—to soften the bolts for later cutting into staves. Originally, there were wooden steam tunnels, but in 1905 new tunnels built of German concrete—which turned out to be of poor quality—were constructed at the end of the downtown mill area.

From the steam tunnels the warm, softened bolts were taken to the workmen who operated special cutting machines. They depressed a pedal and a large knife came down and cut off thin slices from the bolt. These stave "blanks" varied in width depending on the size of the log. The blanks were then either placed in a steam-operated dry kiln or air-dried in the old Albert Lewis mill, and in later years in open sheds. This wood had to be dried to remove moisture and to harden it. As production increased, several wooden sheds, 200-feet long, were built on the opposite side of the creek towards Church Row to air-dry stave blanks.

A separate milling process cut square blanks for future use by coopers as barrel heads and for drying the blanks in the air-sheds, followed by additional drying in a separate kiln. Heat for the kilns was provided by steam piped from a boiler at the stave mill. The staves and heads were dried by radiation from the steam pipes.

Once fully dried, the flat, rectangular stave blanks were again cut into uniform bevelled pieces by "stave cutters." This was called jointing. The final stave piece was wider in the middle than at either end (a barrel bulges at the center). A helper gathered the finished staves and with a press machine packed them fifty at a time and tied the package with a tarred string. A two-man crew cutting and packing could joint 10,000 staves a day, splitting $2.50 each for a day's work. The day's production at the stave mill was 45,000 staves. Stave jointing was hazardous work. Many men and inexperienced boys had fingers cut off in the knifes. The men at

Ranald Douglas took several views of the April 19, 1909, explosion at the Ricketts sawmill.

the stave mill were delighted to horrify frequent mill visitors with a jar of alcohol where the amputated fingers were kept.

Community Life

Housing at Ricketts was leased from Trexler and Turrell. The rates may have varied over time, but a typical charge was $2.50 a month for a four-room house. The first floor would have a kitchen and living area; two bedrooms were on the second floor. The town did not have utility services. Only the sawmill, stave mill, and company store had electricity. The church pastor caused a sensation one winter when he rigged up a flashing electric star for the church Christmas tree. The company houses did not have any indoor plumbing or running water. In fact, only the Turrell home was fitted with plumbing, with water to his home pumped to a storage tank in the attic. Out-houses, of course, were very common. Community wells, and a major spring near the sawmill, provided water for the residents. There was plenty of wood around to chop for firewood, but there was also a hard-coal dump by the railroad trestle near the station to purchase stove coal. But people who purchased coal, rather than chopped wood, were sometimes considered "lazy."

At its height, the town of Ricketts numbered about 800 people. A census was conducted in 1900 and 1910. The census takers in 1910 received 5¢ per person and 25¢ for each farm survey. Because of the travel and expense to cover the North Mountain territory, the census takers also wanted expense money. The government agreed to pay some expense money but reduced the head rate to 3¢ and the farms to 17.5¢. When the census takers asked the Hungarians in the woods how many children they had, a few expressed uncertainty since their wives were still in the "old country" while the Hungarians were in the American woods the last two or three years.

On June 4, 1909, the barrel head manufacturing mill in downtown Ricketts caught fire. The mill was rebuilt. In the left background are air-drying sheds on the opposite side of Mehoopany Creek. The creek cannot be seen in this view. The church is visible in the top center of the Douglas photograph.

Four of Trexler and Turrell's six locomotives are depicted in this work. This Climax (No. 2) locomotive was built in 1893 and was sold to a Texas operation in 1906.

Ricketts was a market place for farmers from "down the mountain" who sold fruit, vegetables, eggs, and milk products. The wagon hucksters would sometimes pick up a child in the town to serve as an interpreter for the farmer as he made his way to the lumber camps. Milk was dipped and sold from cans in a railroad car to women waiting at the Ricketts station with pails.

Local farmers could also find employment in the winter at Ricketts. The company hired the farmers and their horse teams at $5 a day to sled timber down the skid trails to the rail line. Temporary work was also available cutting ice for Lewis and Stull in Mountain Springs and presumably, too, at Lake Ganoga.

An early form of socialized medicine prevailed in the company town. Individual workman paid 50¢ a month and families $1 a month to a fund to maintain a company physician. The physician most remembered was Dr. Kingsley, who also served as the town dentist. Tooth extractions were no problem: two volunteers from the street to hold the patient down and a pair of pliers expertly handled by the "doc" did the job. The community barber, Walker Allen, at least before 1900, was the physician's assistant. Allen rented his shop from the company for $4 a month. Haircuts were 10¢, up to 20¢ for extras. He made $2 or $3 a day. But he joined the army during the Spanish–American War in 1898. After he returned to Ricketts a year later, he sold the business for $100 and rejoined the service.

The managers of the timber tracts had to contend with whatever natural and environmental circumstances occurred. Two substantial problems occurred in the mid-1890s. In late September 1896, a huge storm crossed Florida from the Gulf of Mexico; it followed the east coast to Washington, D.C., where the storm

Trexler and Turrell's Climax (No. 3) is shown at a log landing.

center veered west towards Detroit. There was a severe trough of low pressure north of the storm, and during the afternoon of September 29, a gale began to blow from the southwest over the North Mountain. In the early morning of September 30, between 1:30 and 2:30 a.m., a great windfall swept from the south and tore through the Ricketts tracts. An estimated 200 million feet of timber, for a 30 to 40-mile width, over an area of 15,000 acres, was smashed to the ground. All of the tree tops of the fallen timber pointed north. The Trexler crews tried to salvage the bark and timber, but realized only 80,000 cords, losing an estimated 40,000 cords because of the destruction. Timbering the fallen stock was undoubtedly given priority in the following months.

A major beetle infestation of spruce trees occurred between 1895 and 1896. Spruce began dying shortly after substantial lumbering began in the early 1890s. The blight seemed to have begun below Forkston and spread south to Ricketts and Stull. Apparently, the beetles took hold in the dead stumps and limbs of earlier cuttings, spread to the live timber elsewhere, and rapidly killed the standing trees. The infected trees represented several million board feet of lumber. In 1896, the Trexler and Turrell Company built a second mill—perhaps the Kasson Brook Mill—several miles north of Stull, to quickly save about 2 million feet of their infested tracts. Trexler cut another 9 million feet of diseased trees at Ricketts, with an even greater amount to follow. In Stull, the Lewis company ran roads into the spruce woods to cut and haul dead trees, representing 5 million feet of lumber. These tactics worked well, and within a year the beetle infestation was checked.

There was no police force at Ricketts. At best, a constable—undoubtedly an appointed part-time position—was available. There was also a constable at Lopez, known as a much more rowdy town due to the open availability of beer and alcohol. A quick and rough justice prevailed when there was difficulty. One Saturday, a southerner named Mal Wyris, who had been drinking, was at

A Heisler (No. 4) locomotive was purchased in 1901 and was unusual for the region. It was later used at Big Run where it was wrecked in a runaway accident at Cherry Run.

the Ricketts House and tried to assault Charlie Jackson, a black cook at the hotel, with a knife. An assembling crowd separated them and the incident apparently was forgotten. Later, Wyris appeared again, but this time with a shotgun which was taken away from him. Later in the evening, Wyris chased after a man who left the barber shop, who Wyris thought was Jackson. This time a group of men grabbed Wyris and threw him into an empty railroad car and locked it shut. The freight train left the next day and Wyris never returned.

While Ricketts discouraged drinking, it could not be eliminated. The men would set up shacks in the woods to gather for drinking parties and card-playing—but presumably on Saturday nights and Sundays—the only time they were free. A drunk in town could be locked up in a room overnight at the company store to dry out. But some accounts state that drunks were immediately fired. Labor issues were uncommon and handled on an ad hoc basis. A group of four stave mill workers in charge of the heading room asked the company manager for Saturday afternoons off if they could reach their barrel-head quota by noon. The company concurred; the men met their production standards each week and thereafter had Saturday afternoons free. The rest of the stave mill workers continued to work full Saturdays. But another time a group of men threatened to halt production for an increase in wages, and they were immediately fired.

There were a couple of murders at Ricketts. Sometime about 1905, a domestic-revenge murder occurred. A woman who was a domestic worker for Col. Ricketts in Wilkes-Barre was having difficulty with her husband. The Colonel permitted her to transfer to his Ganoga estate. There she met and began seeing Arthur Potter, a woods crewman. In later weeks, two strangers appeared and made friends with Potter. They persuaded Potter to take them fishing on a boat on a nearby lake. The next morning Potter had disappeared. A friend went to the lake and saw an oar floating in the water. A search party grappled the lake and discovered Potter's body. At first Potter was buried as the victim of an accidental drowning. But doubts lingered and the body was exhumed. A phy-

Trexler's last locomotive Climax (No. 6) weighed 40-45 tons. It, too, was sent to Sonestown at Big Run but apparently it was not used there.

sician found no water in Potter's lungs to indicate drowning and he appeared to have been struck hard behind the left ear. The strangers were located but evidence of murder was inconclusive and a grand jury failed to indict the men.

On January 15, 1914, Charles H. Stanford, a section foreman for the Lehigh Valley Railroad, found George Orr, a laborer for the Lake Ganoga Ice Company, inside Stanford's shanty near the Ricketts railroad station. A quarrel followed and Stanford hit Orr with a double-edged ax, crushing Orr's head, after which Stanford inflicted sixteen additional ax cuts on Orr's body. Some boys heard the fight and called the station agent. Peering through the window, the station agent saw Stanford sitting morosely in a chair and Orr in a pool of blood on the floor.

Constable J. Lawrence Miller and Dr. J.L. Christian from Lopez were called to the scene. At first, Stanford barricaded himself in the shanty, but when Stanford opened the door, Miller grabbed the ax from him and a railroad crew overpowered Stanford. Orr was still alive and was lifted onto a train to be taken to the hospital in Wilkes-Barre, but he died on the way in Bean Run. Stanford claimed Orr tried to steal a watch, but it was more likely Orr had taken food. But there was little sympathy for the quick-tempered Stanford who was not well-liked in the town. Curiously, however, the attack occurred in Wyoming County, the arresting officer was from Sullivan County, and the death occurred in Luzerne County.

There were two substantial disasters at Ricketts, both occurring in the spring of 1909. At about 6:30 a.m. Monday morning, April 19, 1909, the number four boiler at the lumber mill at Ricketts exploded. The night watchman, "Mep" Barnhart, had failed to notice the water had run low in the system, super heating the boilers. He tried to fill the boilers with water too quickly—a known recipe for disaster—and the explosion followed. The debris flew all over town. Rivets from the boiler flew into the trees at Keipertown, a lumber settlement a half-mile from town. The only fatality was H.A. Barnhart, the watchman's brother, who was killed when a brick blown out of the boiler house foundation flew 200 yards and crashed through the roof of George Grimes's porch where Barnhart was standing. The brick hit Barnhart and crushed his skull. A half-century later, during town reunions, former residents still remembered exactly what they were doing when the boiler blew.

Five weeks later, on Friday, June 4, 1909, at 11:30 a.m., the drying kiln at the heading mill in downtown Ricketts caught fire and completely destroyed the mill. Spontaneous combustion, activated within the kiln due to the 250-degree temperature inside, caused a sawdust fire. Debris fell on the cord to the mill whistle and it blew until the steam ran out. Two hundred men tried to dampen the fire which spread over an acre of ground and threatened the stave and grist mills. The fifty men in the plant lost work for a time until the heading mill was rebuilt. An estimated $10,000 in stock was lost.

The End of the Town

In July 1911, an account stated that the Trexler and Turrell mill in Ricketts, improved over the years to a daily capacity of 125,000 board feet, had cut over 500 million feet of lumber since 1890 when the mill opened, five times the estimate made in 1894 for the mill's probable life. Over the years, the log train lines had reached ten miles to the northeast and eight miles south and west of the mill. At this time, Trexler and Turrell were operating three locomotives over 22 miles of logging tracks utilizing about 62 logging cars. Production was 80,000 feet daily, less than capacity and diminishing rapidly. Only one more year of timber tract was left to serve Ricketts, unless the Trexler company could secure another tract thirteen miles away from the Central Pennsylvania Lumber Company, a conglomerate which began operations in the region in 1903.

In August 1912, Adam Schoch was in charge of the sawmill, with J.C. Cornell as foreman of the stave and heading mills. William May was chief clerk at the company store, with Emery Schock as the store bookkeeper. G.J. Heintzelman was still the postmaster and Trexler and Turrell accountant for the town. G.N. Peet, the former Ricketts blacksmith, had moved to Lopez.

The last full season of lumbering was in 1913. The final tract cut by Trexler and Turrell was in the Cherry Ridge section located

The Ganoga log-built station is on the left while a carload of rough cut lumber sits idle.

northeast of Lake Jean. The company was unable to obtain additional tracts from the Central Pennsylvania Lumber Company, which itself wanted to expand near the Ricketts area. By the fall of 1913, Trexler finished stave cutting at the Ricketts mill, and the company closed its operations. By the end of 1914, the town was nearly deserted and only five families still lived there.

As Ricketts closed, Trexler and Turrell continued a small mill operation at South Mountain above Noxen, at least through 1914. The Trexlers and J.E. Turrell joined with Col. Ricketts to form the Big Run Manufacturing Company (1914–1922) at Sonestown at the mouth of Big Run further west in Sullivan County. Col. Ricketts held a 20 percent interest in the Big Run company. The company made sugar barrel staves and heads. The company transferred its number four Heisler, number five Shay, and number six Climax locomotives from Ricketts to Big Run, but the Climax may not have been used there. Big Run employed about eighty men, some of whom transferred from Ricketts. The Big Run operation closed three years after Col. Ricketts' death. The Trexler firm did not continue operations elsewhere in North Mountain after Big Run. H.C. Trexler and his family associates, of course, had massive industrial and commercial operations in Allentown where they were headquartered. Indeed, North Mountain was a relatively small enterprise for Harry C. Trexler compared to his other Lehigh Valley enterprises.

Afterword

The timbering profits of Col. Ricketts and the Trexler and Turrell company from timbering on the Ricketts lands cannot be determined since the business records have not survived. It appears that the Colonel received $30,000 annually from the Trexler company for timbering rights, at least through 1896. If this arrangement continued, the Colonel may have earned $720,000 during the 24 years lumbering occurred from 1890 to 1913, not too removed from the proceeds promised to Col. Ricketts if the "English deal" had succeeded. There is also evidence in the Ricketts' estate records that he held a 25 percent interest in the Trexler and Turrell Lumber Company, which would have realized additional income to him from the Ricketts lumbering operations.

Unfortunately, Col. Ricketts lost significant capital in a failing effort to develop hydro-electric power at two lakes he owned in Ricketts Glen. Lake Rose, south of Lake Jean, was built on the west branch of Kitchen's Creek as a log splash pond by a squatter named Jesse Dodson, who cut cherry trees to make bedsteads (c. 1830–1860). These were hauled to Pottsville and Reading for sale. The lake's early name was Dodson's Dam. In 1905, Ricketts reinforced the Lake Rose dam. The name "Rose" was a Ricketts family name in Scotland. The family can be traced to Kilvarock Castle, in Nairn, Scotland.

Granville Heintzelman, the Ricketts company bookkeeper, with his family and automobile, a rarity at Ricketts, circa 1910.

Ricketts also built a concrete dam on the east or Sickler branch of Kitchen Creek to create Lake Leigh, another Ricketts family name which was carried by the Colonel's second daughter. The concrete dam was on the site of an earlier log dam built by a squatter named Sickler, who also cut cherry for bedsteads (c. 1838–1860). But the Lake Rose and Lake Leigh dams were poorly constructed and could not be used for hydro-electric purposes. Fifty years later, Lake Leigh and Lake Rose were condemned by the state and are now drained.

Dodson also built Timber Dam on Kitchen Creek below a small lake called Mud Pond. Colonel Ricketts reinforced the dam in 1905 and named it Lake Jean after his first daughter. In 1949, the Department of Forests and Waters replaced the log dam at Lake Jean with a larger earth-filled dam with dikes at the east and west ends. The enlarged lake also enclosed former Mud Pond to create a 245-acre Lake Jean.

While Ricketts, Lopez, and Jamison City were in operation, a consolidation of lumbering operations in the state occurred with the creation of the Central Pennsylvania Lumber Company (1903–1941). The Central Pennsylvania company was an outgrowth of the United States Leather Company, which was formed in 1893 to consolidate the tanning industry. In our region it owned the Union, Elk, and Penn Tanning Companies. In 1903, the tanning companies formed the Central Pennsylvania Lumber Company to purchase timberlands and mills. It eventually controlled sixteen mills in seven northcentral Pennsylvania counties, including Jamison City in Columbia County and the Masten and Laquin mills in Bradford County. For a time after the town of Ricketts closed, the Central Pennsylvania company leased from Col. Ricketts a portion of a former Trexler and Turrell logging track outside the town of Ricketts, apparently to reach an isolated section of timberland, which was presumably milled at Laquin in Bradford County.

In March and December 1924, the Central Pennsylvania Lumber Company sold 12,500 acres in Davidson Township, Sullivan County, to the Commonwealth of Pennsylvania for state game lands. These lands were purchased by Central Pennsylvania Lumber from the Union Tannery Company in 1903 and the Elk Tanning Company in 1921, and they were formerly the North Mountain Lumber Company tracts purchased in 1889 for the Jamison City lumbering operation. They were the Jamison syndicate lands which were to have been combined with Col. Ricketts' 45,000 acres in the "English Deal" in 1888–1889. They became a main source for State Game Lands No. 13 west of Ricketts Glen.

The Ricketts Estate

Col. Robert Bruce Ricketts and Elizabeth Reynolds Ricketts were survived by three children. Jean Holberton Ricketts (1873–1929) never married. A second daughter, Frances Leigh Ricketts (1881–1970), married Judge William S. McLean, Jr., (1877–1938) in 1921.

The Colonel's son, William Reynolds Ricketts (1869–1956), was generally associated with the Ricketts holdings after his father's death. An 1892 graduate of Yale University, William R. Ricketts was engaged with his father in the management of the Ricketts enterprises. He was the volunteer curator of mineralogy of the Wyoming Historical and Geological Society, a world-class stamp collector, and an avid mystery book fan and collector. He married Stella Shoemaker from Forty Fort, Pennsylvania, and they had a son Robert Bruce Ricketts, II (1907–1927), who died of typhoid fever while attending Los Alamos Ranch School in Santa Fe, New Mexico. After the death of Stella Shoemaker Ricketts in 1909 at age 32, William R. Ricketts married Margaret Beach (1881–1950) from Ballston Spa, New York.

Four of these family members, Jean H. Ricketts, R. Bruce Ricketts, II, Margaret B. Ricketts, and William R. Ricketts are buried in the family cemetery at Lake Ganoga. John Green, the Colonel's servant, is also buried there.

On August 1, 1941, Governor Arthur L. James, a native of Plymouth, signed legislation authorizing the state to acquire the Ricketts lands in Luzerne and Sullivan Counties for $150,000 for state park and game lands. In December 1942, the Ricketts heirs sold the 1,261-acre tract which encompasses the Kitchen Creek glens and waterfalls to the state for $82,000. The glens are the heart of Ricketts Glen State Park in Fairmont Township in Luzerne County. In December 1945 and September 1950, the Ricketts heirs sold another 16,000 acres in the two counties to the state for $68,000.

Ricketts Glen State Park is comprised of about 10,000 acres formerly owned by the Ricketts family, and 3,050 acres purchased from other persons. The balance of the Ricketts lands were incorporated into the surrounding game lands.

In October 1957, the 3,140-acre tract which comprises the Lake Ganoga lands, including the Stone House, were sold for $109,000 to trustees who formed the Lake Ganoga Association in September 1959 to regulate and preserve the recreation and residential facilities at Lake Ganoga. The Department of Forests and Waters had bid on the tract but the state offer was inadequate to purchase the lands.

The Stull Lands

When the Albert Lewis and Arthur L. Stull partnership was dissolved in 1912, Lewis had retained ownership of 15,000 acres in Wyoming and Luzerne counties. In January 1927, the Lewis heirs transferred these lands, plus additional lands in Dallas and Lake Townships, to the brothers Arthur L. Stull and Albert A. Stull. With this sale, the Lewis estate divested itself of all lands Albert Lewis formerly held on the west side of the Susquehanna River.

Between 1930 and 1934, the Stulls transferred 5,840 acres of Wyoming County lands to the Pennsylvania Game Commission. In 1938, an 82-acre site for a children's camp at Noxen was transferred by Albert A. Stull to a Wilkes-Barre charity. The lots were sold to private interests between 1979 and 1985. In June 1942, the Arthur L. Stull Company and the Stull heirs sold 2,283 acres in Ross and Fairmont Townships to T.N. Wood. These lands surrounded, but did not include, the ice plants at the two splash dams. Wood sold this property in December 1947 to the State Game Commission. These lands, except for the former children's camp, form the core of State Game Lands No. 57 adjacent to Ricketts Glen State Park.

In July 1943, the Stulls contracted with Ralph S. Smith and Gordon Smith, partners in the Crawford Smith Lumber Company, to timber 6,700 acres in Fairmont, Ross, and Lake Townships in Luzerne County. In November 1963, the Stull heirs sold these tracts to the Crawford Smith Company. These tracts represented substantially all of the remaining Stull land interests. Since 1963, Crawford Smith acreage has been sold to private interests or are still reserved by the Crawford Smith estate.

In May 1953, five years after the last ice-cutting season in Mountain Springs, R.A. Davis and John W. White, who acquired Mountain Springs from the Stulls in 1945, sold the 368-acre site which contained Splash Dams No. 1 and 2, to F.T. Butler, an agent for Donald P. Morgan and Emil C. Wagner, who in turn sold the tract in July 1959 to the Pennsylvania Fish Commission. Splash Dam No. 1 was condemned and drained in 1957. Splash Dam No. 2 was rebuilt as a concrete dam and enlarged in 1957. Renamed Mount Springs Lake by the Fish Commission, it was regularly stocked with trout, but acid rain conditions have ruined the lake and stocking has been discontinued. In July 1953, the Lehigh Valley Railroad sold the Bowman's Creek railroad bed through the game lands to the state, and the Fish Commission now maintains it from Noxen to Ricketts.

The Lewis Estate

Albert Lewis was survived by his widow Lily C. Lewis (1868–1950), a daughter Lily (Wiffie) Lewis Seneff (1896–1971), and a son Hugh (Dick) Romaine Lewis (1895–1948). Another son, George Lewis, died in infancy. A third son, Albert (Bert) Lewis, Jr. (1893–1916), held promise as his father's business heir but tragically died at age 23 from a head injury after falling from a railroad hand car which overturned after striking an object on the track.

The Bear Creek Ice Company property was transferred in November 1931 by Lily C. Lewis to Burt A. Bryant, who incorporated another Bear Creek Ice Company with D.S. Lauderbaugh and John T. Williams as partners. But the new company only lasted one year before the property reverted by sale to Lewis's daughter, Lily Lewis (Kilner), in December 1932. For another year, the Bear Creek ice operations were leased to Lauderbaugh, then for the last four years to R.A. Davis, before closing in 1938.

The 30,000 acres of Lewis lands in Bear Creek and surrounding townships were partitioned among the Lewis heirs in litigation which began in 1930 and concluded in late 1942. The lands were divided among the three heirs, and since that time they have been privately developed.

The Bear Creek dam and lake which once served the Lewis ice industry, and the second Lewis country mansion adjacent to the Bear Creek dam on Route 315, always catch the eye of the traveler. In the surrounding woods, there are other reminders of the Lewis era: the family cemetery, Grace Chapel, the village workers' church, and the lovely trails and woods which still surround the old company village.

F. Charles Petrillo is a graduate of Wilkes College, Wilkes-Barre, Pennsylvania, and the Dickinson School of Law, Carlisle, Pennsylvania. He is the author of *Harvey's Lake,* published in 1983, and *Anthracite and Slackwater: The North Branch Canal 1828–1901,* published in 1986. He is an officer and chair of committees for the Wyoming Historical and Geological Society in Wilkes-Barre.